Row upon Row

Sea Grass Baskets
of the South Carolina Lowcountry

by Dale Rosengarten

Lynn Robertson Myers
Project Director

McKissick Museum
University of South Carolina

This publication is the result of a documentation and exhibition project
funded in part by the National Endowment for the Arts, Folk Arts Program.

All photographs, unless otherwise
indicated, are by Will Barnes and
reproduced courtesy of the McKissick
Museum.
Photographic Credits:
Jan Arnow: cover, 43a, 54
Brookgreen Gardens, Murrells Inlet, South Carolina: 24b, 25a
Carolina Art Association/Gibbes Art Gallery, Charleston, South Carolina:
vi, vii, 20a, 25b, 26b, 47a
Charleston Museum, Charleston, South Carolina: 20b
Jannie Cohen: 33a
John Coles: 47b
Greg Day: 9a, 13bc, 36a, 37a
Susan Dugan: 14a, 32b, 38
Francis Marion National Forest, McClellanville, South Carolina: 8, 37b
Louise Johnson Guy: 39a
John E. Huguley: 10, 34b
Clifford L. Legerton:33b, 34a, 35
Library of Congress, Archives of Folk Culture: 31b
John McWilliams: 11a, 46
New York Historical Society, New York, New York: 21a, 24a
The Rice Museum, Georgetown, South Carolina: 9b
Dale Rosengarten: 12, 15ac, 32a, 40a, 43b, 44a, 62, 72
Theodore Rosengarten: 11b, 12a, 17a, 36b
Smithsonian Institution, National Museum of American History, Division of
Community Life: 16b
South Carolina Arts Commission, Columbia, South Carolina: 45ac
South Carolina Educational Television, Columbia, South Carolina: 39b, 44c
South Carolina Historical Society, Charleston, South Carolina: 23b, 26a
South Caroliniana Library, University of South Carolina, Columbia, South
Carolina: 26c, 29b, 30b
Southern Historical Collection, University of North Carolina Library, Penn
School Historical Collection, Chapel Hill, North Carolina (with permission
of Penn Community Services, Inc.): 27b, 28, 29a, 30a
Gary Stanton: 31a
Darcy Wingfield: 41, 44b, 45b, 64

Library of Congress Publication Data:
Rosengarten, Dale, 1948
        Row Upon Row: Sea Grass Baskets of the South
        Carolina Lowcountry
Bibliography: p. 65
1. Folk Art, Afro-American-South Carolina-essay.
        I. McKissick Museum. II. Title.
TT879.B3R65 1986 746.41'2'0899607307579 86-61725
ISBN 0-938983-02-4

Row Upon Row: Sea Grass Baskets
of the South Carolina Lowcountry

Organized by the McKissick Museum, University of South Carolina as part of its program to document and promote Southern Folk Arts.

Catherine Wilson Horne, Exhibition Curator.

This travelling exhibition is supported by the National Endowment for the Humanities.

Exhibition Itinerary

Museum of York County
Rock Hill, South Carolina
October 10, 1987 - January 2, 1988

The Columbus Museum
Columbus, Georgia
February 1, 1988 - April 12, 1988

Gibbes Art Gallery
Charleston, South Carolina
August 16, 1988 - October 25, 1988

California Afro-American Museum
Los Angeles, California
November 22, 1988 - February 1, 1989

Durham Arts Council
Durham, North Carolina
June 8, 1989 - August 16, 1989

Decorative Arts Museum
Arkansas Arts Center
Little Rock, Arkansas
September 14, 1989 - November 22, 1989

Flint Institute of Art
Flint, Michigan
December 20, 1989 - February 28, 1990

Ten years ago I sat in a University office listening to an interviewee for a grant funded project tell the director of the Museum why she wanted to spend a year researching South Carolina sea grass baskets. Little did the three of us— myself, George Terry, and Dale Rosengarten—know what an impact this work would have on not only our professional lives and the future of the Museum but also on the revival of this important craft. Today, Ms. Rosengarten is still actively researching and lecturing on sea grass baskets. McKissick Museum is deeply involved in numerous projects to promote an understanding of regional folklife. Included in this is a research and exhibition project focusing on how such institutions as the Penn Normal Industrial and Agricultural School, through their teaching of basketry, helped create our concept of Southern craft. During the years inbetween the original start of our venture into documenting these baskets and now, McKissick Museum has travelled the exhibition, *Row Upon Row*, to dozens of museums and cultural centers across the United States, sponsored a conference on the importance of keeping this craft as a flourishing part of the lowcountry community, helped with transplantation projects to increase the availability of grasses, and distributed thousands of brochures on the history of these baskets.

In his introduction to the 1987 edition, Dr. Terry, then director of McKissick Museum and now Vice Provost and Dean of Libraries and Information Systems, raised the question, "whether folk artists such as sea grass basketmakers can sustain their creative capacity in the face of contemporary tastes and intense real estate development." I am happy to report that ten years and one major hurricane later, the art form seems to be flourishing. There is an active association of sea grass basketmakers that provides support to its members as well as public information on the craft to the hundreds of inquiries that come in from across the United States. Resort owners and city officials throughout the lowcountry have become aware of the benefit of this local tradition, and "cultural tourism" has become a recognized priority of the State's department of Parks, Recreation and Tourism. Dozens of basketmakers can be found selling their creations at the Charleston market or in the community of Mt. Pleasant. Individual basketmakers have been recognized for the excellence of their skills and included in regional and national exhibitions. But most important of all, a new generation of Americans has become aware that these objects are an important and visible link in our cultural ties to an African past. As the prophetic statement made by one of the basketmakers says ". . . time will come, they will sew." And by their sewing, the rest of us have the benefit of this rich tradition.

Lynn Robertson
Executive Director
McKissick Museum

Introduction

South Carolina has always enjoyed a rich heritage of folk traditions largely due to the early cultural interaction of diverse African, European, and Native American peoples in the lowcountry region. As the plantation system came to dominate Carolina's social and economic development, some ethnic traditions became less distinct. But those traditions that remained intact during the eighteenth century creolization of South Carolina's lowcountry society are responsible for much of the distinctive folk art produced in that area. Among the most readily identifiable products of this cultural tenacity are the coiled sea grass baskets produced along the Southeastern coast. They belong to a basketsewing tradition—centered today in the small community of Mt. Pleasant just north of Charleston—that has survived in America for over three hundred years.

Row Upon Row: Sea Grass Baskets of the Lowcountry is part of an in-depth study of this folk art form. Eighteen months of intensive investigation included both research into the history of the still flourishing African American craft and a survey of its current status. While this coiled basket tradition has evolved over the past century from an agricultural craft to an art form produced for sale, there remains a strong sense of continuity and family tradition. Besides examining documentary materials such as plantation records, diaries, wills, and old photographs, much of the study was devoted to the craft as it is practiced today. Nearly forty contemporary basketmakers were interviewed by Dale Rosengarten with regard to their aesthetic approach to the craft and what changes in the tradition they had witnessed in their lifetimes. Each individual's techniques and favored styles were examined. In addition, the role of the basketmaker's family in transmitting the tradition was studied. McKissick's investigation has yielded the first full-scale description of the history of this important folk art. Comparisons of old baskets with current techniques, styles, and materials indicate that this craft has undergone sometimes subtle and sometimes striking changes during its development in South Carolina.

An important goal of this project has been to describe how cultural and economic events have effected the baskets and their makers. Though the creation of folk art can be considered a personal statement, it is also the response to a demand. The early forms of this craft were determined by the introduction of the rice culture into the plantation economy. Processing this grain required a variety of tools, including the fanner basket, which was used to throw the pounded grain into the air, allowing the wind to blow away the chaff.

Small farms acquired by black families after the Civil War demanded a variety of household baskets. By the end of the nineteenth century the coiled sea grass basket began gaining recognition as an important African American art form. This transformation coincided with the Art and Crafts Movement of the turn of the century and the introduction of "Native Island Basketry" into the curriculum at the Penn Normal, Industrial and Agricultural School in 1904. It was during this period, Ms. Rosengarten points out, that new shapes derived from traditional basket forms started to appear.

The twentieth century brought the demands of a consumer society to the basketmakers, as sewers began to sell their wares on the road or through mail order outlets and gift shops. Especially in Mt. Pleasant the craft was revitalized, and a number of shapes and styles were introduced to cater to Charleston's thriving tourist industry. Merchants and middlemen who bought baskets in quantity for resale modified the long tradition of this craft by making special requests and providing specifications which would make baskets more marketable. Their chief influence, however, was in disseminating examples of the craft and in helping to create an audience.

Watercolor Study by Alice R. H. Smith

The appearance of basket stands along Highway 17 was instrumental in popularizing coiled basketry during the first half of the twentieth century. Intended to allow sewers to compete in the retail market, the stands established direct contact between maker and buyer and encouraged artists to develop new forms of their own. The pressures of modernization have also altered the material and techniques used by the basketmakers. Agricultural work baskets, Ms. Rosengarten explains, were made most often from black rush bound with oak splits or strips of palmetto stem. As the market for household baskets developed, Mt. Pleasant makers turned exclusively to sweetgrass, decorated with longleaf pine needles and sewn with strips of palmetto leaf. In recent years sweetgrass has become difficult to obtain and rush is coming into use again.

Today, the question remains to be answered whether folk artists such as sea grass basketmakers can sustain their creative capacity in the face of contemporary consumer tastes and intense real estate development. The various forms created by a sewer through technical mastery are reflections of the community which created the tradition and which has seen it through complex economic, social, and cultural changes. For early sewers, economy of means was the dominant factor and even decoration was secondary to practicality. Today's baskets are never merely useful. Use aside, they reveal a world inhabited by thoughtful people and express a finely developed social order. It was with this idea in mind that McKissick Museum undertook this project and selected Ms. Rosengarten as its guest curator.

The persistence of the coiled sea grass basket tradition over a span of three centuries is a tribute to the African American basketmakers who value their craft as an important part of their cultural heritage and as a means of self-expression. The tradition faces many challenges from increasing modernization in the lowcountry. As better economic opportunities arise, daughters undoubtedly will turn away from the craft of their mothers and grandmothers to pursue more profitable work. But, according to one basketmaker reflecting on whether her children will continue the tradition, "It may be hard for them to see it, but days will come when they will sew baskets . . . This basket here is strictly just in the lowcountry, and if the generation don't take it up when we gone, it's going to die away. But, they will sew baskets. They will, time will come, they will sew."

George D. Terry
Director
McKissick Museum

Watercolor Study by Alice R. H. Smith

Basket Stand, 1938

Row Upon Row
Sea Grass Baskets of the South Carolina Lowcountry

Coiled sea grass basketry flourishes today in the tidewater region of South Carolina. In all seasons, on any given day, travellers to Charleston can find dozens of basketmakers from the suburban community of Mt. Pleasant, showing their wares on street corners in the city and on crudely constructed stands along Highway 17. On Market Street and the corners of Meeting and Broad, arrays of baskets in a multitude of shapes and sizes grace the edge of the sidewalks, while their makers sit behind them, talking and sewing new forms. North of the historic city, across the Cooper River Bridge, as you drive past the shopping malls and subdivisions that have sprouted like mushrooms in Mt. Pleasant, you might not know which state you were in, if it weren't for the palmetto trees and the basket stands.

Contemporary Mt. Pleasant baskets descend from an ancient African folk art that was introduced in Carolina late in the seventeenth century. The African peoples who were brought to America to cultivate rice and other crops carried with them skills they had used in everyday life. Pottery and woodcarving, boatbuilding and netmaking, as well as speech patterns, folk songs, and musical instruments, all survived the Atlantic passage and resurfaced in new plantation communities. In the lowcountry, where blacks outnumbered whites as early as 1708, coiled basketry was one of several viable African "carryovers."

Evolution of Forms

The early history of African American basketry parallels the rise of rice cultivation on the southeastern coast. Even before Carolina was colonized, rice had been proposed as a staple for export. Around 1690, after two decades of experimentation, settlers began producing a "plausible yield,"[1] and by the mid-eighteenth century, rice was the principal crop of what was to become the wealthiest group of planters in America. From the start, lowcountry plantations proved to be friendly environments for the production of African American sea grass baskets. Indeed,

rice could not have been processed without a particular coiled basket, called the "fanner." The fanner was a wide winnowing tray used to "fan" rice—that is, to throw the threshed and pounded grain into the air or drop it from a basket held at a height into another basket, allowing the wind to blow away the chaff.

Utilizing the natural materials of their new environment, African Americans made fanners and other large agricultural baskets out of black rush, an abundant marsh grass, bound with thin splits of white oak or strips from the stem of the saw palmetto. As rice culture spread, so did the manufacture of these coiled work baskets. After the Civil War, men and some women continued to sew rush baskets for use on those plantations which weathered Reconstruction, and on small, family farms which were carved out of the old estates.

The anonymous nature of early African American basketry belies its range and importance. At one time the craft must have been practiced along the whole length of the coastal rice kingdom, from its southernmost outposts on the St. Johns River, in Florida, to its northern reaches near Cape Fear, North Carolina.[2] Nine-tenths of the antebellum rice crop was grown in South Carolina and Georgia, however, and it is here that sea grass baskets have left a historical record. It is easy to see why coiled basketry persisted along rice-growing tidal rivers, yet it also took firm hold on those Sea Islands where commercial quantities of rice were not produced. There, rice was cultivated as a provision crop, for local consumption; slaves from rice-growing regions of Africa were said to "languish without their favorite food."[3] The dietary preferences of African Americans were, in some cases, as important as the profit motives of their masters in determining whether coiled baskets would be made. Well into the 1900s, black farmers throughout the lowcountry planted small crops of "upland" or "dry" rice and processed the grain in the African way, using flails, mortars and pestles, and fanner baskets.

Despite the coiled basket's steady use as an implement of American rice culture and as a common household object, it is difficult to assemble a precise history of the craft. Because grasses and wood fibers are highly perishable

Fanning Rice, 1977

Fanning Rice at Wedgefield Plantation, ca. 1890

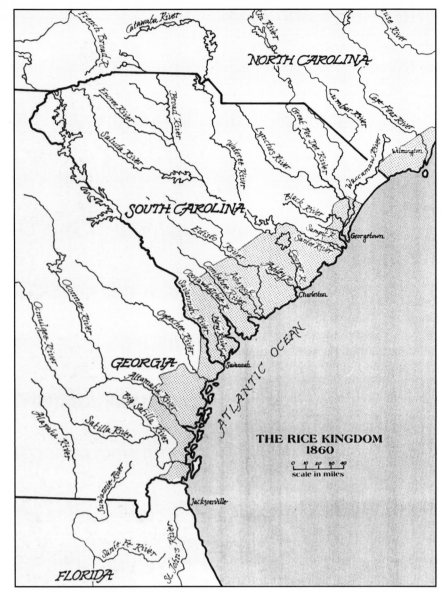

The Rice Kingdom   Kerry O'Connor Hood

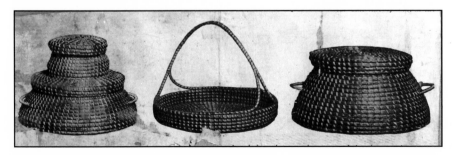

Baskets Illustrated by the Seagrass Basket Company, ca. 1920

skill of the maker, and whether he or she was right-handed or left-handed. But the fragments are mute on the subject of who made them, when, and where.

A revolution in materials, forms, and functions occurred at the turn of the twentieth century in Mt. Pleasant, where a community of landed black families began mass-producing and selling "show baskets" made of sweetgrass. Sweetgrass baskets had been sewn before, but never on a scale to rival rush handwork. During the agricultural depressions following the hurricanes of the 1890s and early 1900s and the arrival of the boll weevil in 1918, show baskets provided a source of cash. Mt. Pleasant basketmakers and Charleston retailers alike saw possibilities in a new and growing tourist market. Sweetgrass baskets, sewn with strips of palmetto leaf and adorned with longleaf pine needles, became a local specialty, and women came to dominate the craft.

While Mt. Pleasant sewers turned their talents to sweetgrass, rush work baskets continued to be made in isolated communities along the coast of South Carolina and Georgia. At the Penn School, on St. Helena Island, "Native Island Basketry" remained an important part of the "industrial" curriculum for fifty years. But as agriculture declined and resort development began to alter the face of the lowcountry, rush baskets went out of use and almost disappeared. In recent years, however, sweetgrass has become increasingly scarce around Charleston and Mt. Pleasant. Rush is making a comeback—not as the sole material in baskets, but as an element incorporated with sweetgrass to add strength and color to large sculptural forms.

Natural Materials

The lowcountry is a country of grasses. Historically, basketmakers have gathered from the coastal *flora* a number of wild grasses and cultivated plants. Spartina, broomsedge, rice straw, and twisted corn shucks at times were used in place of rush, but rush was by far the preferred material in early coiled baskets. Basketmakers today appreciate the grass for its rich golden color, durability, large gauge, and light weight, as well as for its accessibility.

Black rush (*Juncus roemerianus*), known locally as "bulrush," "rushel," or "needlegrass," is tolerant of varying salinity levels but grows

and wear out in normal use, and because they lack the intrinsic value of porcelain or silver, discarded baskets in early times were assigned to the woodpile or left to rot in the shed. Surviving examples of old baskets reveal sharp regional differences and subtle individual variations. We can determine what materials these artifacts were made from, the degree of

most abundantly in lowlands intermittently exposed to tidal flooding. Rooted in the marsh, exposed to sun, strong winds, salt spray, and high tides, bulrush is tough—tougher than sweetgrass but rougher on the hands and more difficult to bind tightly. Rush is cut green with the curved blade of a "rice" or "reef" hook, or with a straight-bladed knife. Contemporary sewers add bulrush to the inside of their rows for strength or use it alternately with sweetgrass. An occasional old-timer will insist that rush and sweetgrass should not be sewn in the same basket,[4] but even these purists begin their rush baskets with knots made of sweetgrass or pine straw.

Sweetgrass (*Muhlenbergia filipes* or *M. capillaris*), prized so highly by Mt. Pleasant sewers, is a long-stemmed plant that grows in tufts behind the second dune line from the ocean or along the boundaries between marsh and woods. Here, salt-tolerant trees and shrubs have pinned down the sand and stopped it from shifting, creating a stable barrier from tidal flooding. All spring and summer, gatherers "pull" the sweetgrass, which slips out of its roots like knives from sheaths. Bundles of grass are then spread in the sun to dry. Used green, they will shrink and make a loose basket. Sweetgrass pales in a day, and soon turns straw-colored. In old baskets it mellows to a deep ochre.

Whether *Muhlenbergia filipes* is a variety of *M. capillaris* or a valid species has long been a subject of dispute among botanists.[5] The current consensus seems to favor the theory of distinct species. All experienced Mt. Pleasant basketmakers describe two kinds of sweetgrass. "The difference between the two straws," Louise White explains, is that one "will grow near to the sea, salt water part. It's heavy grass, kind of fat. And the fresh water grass grow up in the woods. They are very soft and tiny."[6] This second sort—*M. capillaris*—produces long blades of grass which are of such a fine gauge that they must be sewn especially tightly to make a firm basket.

Since contemporary baskets are intended for light household uses and for display, the materials that go into them can afford to be delicate. Strips of the leaves of palm (*Sabal palmetto*) used to sew show baskets are not as durable as the splits of white oak (*Quercus alba*) or of saw palmetto (*Serenoa repens*) used in work baskets. Mt. Pleasant basketmakers switched to palm leaf because it is simpler to prepare, brighter in color, and more pliable than oak. They test individual strips for strength to insure that the palm won't "pop" when it is wrapped around the grass and pulled taut.

The needles of longleaf pine (*Pinus palustris*) which decorate show baskets generally are gathered dry; they provide a russet contrast to the more yellow sweetgrass. Mt. Pleasant sewers began experimenting with this new material around 1920, and it quickly became a staple of the craft. Today most sweetgrass baskets contain some pinestraw, and basketmakers are beginning to use it in conjunction with rush, to create a subtle change of tone and radical change of texture.

Techniques and Tools

Coiling, unlike other basketry techniques, is a process of sewing or stitching. Materials called the *foundation* are sewn together with a stitching element called the *binder* or *weaver*. A *bundle* is the collection of foundation material bound together in one row of a basket. The bundle must be constantly "fed" with new grasses to maintain a continuous foundation of uniform thickness, spiraling out from the center of the basket.

The sturdy bundle of grasses is held together by a relatively thin, flexible binder, which also must be spliced as the sewing progresses. The regularity of stitches, so often admired, is less difficult to achieve than a smooth-flowing, energetic contour. In plaited and twined baskets, contours result largely from elements bent and held in tension. In coiled baskets, the shape is created by building the foundation, row upon row. The process is slow and deliberate and requires a remarkable continuity of precision.[7]

The most problematic part of a coiled basket is the beginning, where the foundation commences. The way a coil is started depends first of all on whether the basket will be oblong or round. For oblong baskets, a length of either rush or sweetgrass is wrapped with carefully spaced stitches, then doubled back on itself, making a second row which is sewn onto the first. The second row is then bent around and stitched onto the other side of the first row.

Round baskets sometimes are started with a short length of foundation doubled back on itself, but usually they are begun by tying the grass in an overhand knot. To tie a knot with a rigid material like rush, old-time basketsewers might soak it in water, or shred the blades lengthwise into finer strands, to make the bundle more flexible.[8] Occasionally,

Mary Jackson Cutting Rush

Joseph Foreman Carrying a Bundle of Rush

Joseph Foreman Pulling Sweetgrass

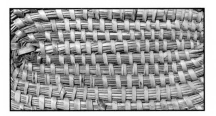

Detail: Oblong Basket (Cat. 14)

Sea Island Knot, Fanner Basket (Cat. 7)

Santee Knot, Fanner Basket (Cat. 2)

they would begin a basket with a more pliable foundation like twisted corn shucks, feeding straw into the bundle when the coil was well underway.

In old work baskets the type of knot may provide a clue to where the baskets were made. On mainland plantations, basketmakers usually tied a knot in the bundle of rush, brought together *both* ends of the bundle, bent it around the knot, and stitched it in place. On the Sea Islands, *one* end of the grass bundle was coiled around and sewn onto the knot. After a second or third row was sewn, the free end of the grass that emerged from the center was cut off blunt, flush with the plane of the basket bottom, and facing *up* as the basket lay in the sewer's lap.

Traditional rush baskets were bound most commonly with oak splits. These thin, narrow weavers were split from white oak boles by the same laborious process required to make splints for oak baskets.[9] Oak binders may be regarded as a distinctly *American* element in African American coiled basketry. European-American basketmakers also adopted white oak in place of Old World materials. Round oak rods supplanted willow in some wickerwork, flat oak splits were used for nearly all splintwork, and oak weavers bound most coiled rye straw baskets.[10]

In place of oak splits, some mainland and all Sea Island basketmakers sewed their rows with strips from the stem of the saw palmetto. To prepare these binders, the outer layer or skin of the stalk was peeled off with a knife and laid across the knees, the smooth, green side resting on a burlap sack or other heavy fabric. Then the pithy core of the stem was scraped away and the skin split lengthwise into narrow weavers. These were dried briefly in the sun and stored in pails of fresh water, to keep them supple.

To add a binder, whether of oak or palmetto butt, the new strip was tied onto the preceding stitch and passed through a stitch in the underlying row. These interlocked stitches curve out from the center of the basket back toward the rim.

To start a round basket in sweetgrass, Mt. Pleasant basketsewers first twist the bundle tightly, holding the "heads," or root ends, of the grass in their teeth. They then tie a knot and begin the coil. Because pine needles are more supple than sweetgrass, contemporary sewers often choose to tie their knots with pine. To make a strong bottom, a heavier foundation material is then fed into the pine bundle.

Today's Mt. Pleasant basketmakers sew exclusively with strips from a leaf of the palmetto tree or cabbage palm. Only the new, unopened frond is used, cut from the center of the tree with a knife. The "fan o'metta" is allowed to dry slightly. Then the sections or "slabs" are pulled apart and the tough edges or "butts" are trimmed off from "head" to "tail"—from the thicker end which grows from the stem to the thinner outer edge of the leaf. Once the sections of leaf are split lengthwise into quarter-inch strips for sewing, and the heads clipped with scissors into points, the strips are placed in plastic bags so they will remain "green" and flexible. They can be kept in a refrigerator or freezer for many months. Before the advent of ice boxes, basketmakers stored their "palm" in a cool spot, stripping only as much as they could use in a short time.

For splitting the palmetto into strips, and for making a space in the coil through which to pull the palm binder, basketmakers use a sewing awl they call a "bone" or a "nail-bone." Earlier sewers made this tool from an actual animal bone—the rib of a cow or, occasionally, the rib of a hog or the bone of a wild animal.[11] Nowadays, most Mt. Pleasant basketmakers make their bones from metal teaspoons. They break off the bowl, hammer the neck flat and file it to a rounded point, then smooth and polish the surface by thrusting it repeatedly into the dirt. Though teaspoons are preferred, almost any sharp metal object will do—a twenty-penny nail, its point flattened and filed smooth, a nail file, or broken scissors. Regardless of what it is made from, the tool is still called a "bone." Many sewers become attached to a special bone and feel uncomfortable using any other. "If you don't have that special one you in trouble," confided Louise White. "Ain't nothing goin' to satisfy your mind." Another sewer, Marie Manigault, stated flatly, "This one I made myself is a teaspoon handle and if I don't have that I don't work. That's my favorite one and I only have one. If I lose that I'd feel lost. I can't work with any kind of tool." The record for longevity of a bone is held by Florence Mazyck, who managed to keep her favorite tool for thirty-seven years.[12]

On the Sea Islands there seems to have been greater variety and more individuality in sewing tools. George Brown, who taught basketmaking at the Penn School on St. Helena for more than three decades, sewed with a bagging needle about four inches long, curved at the point. He ordered these needles by the box, using them also to stitch up the burlap bags in which Penn School baskets, sometimes containing a spray of mistletoe, were shipped to fill mail orders. Brown would thread a string through the eye of the needle and tie it around his wrist to keep it close at hand.[13] On Hilton Head, basketmakers have used pocket knives, ice picks, and other utensils as sewing awls.

All these tools serve the same function—to make a space for the binder to pass through the foundation. The stitching technique differs, however, depending on the basket type and binding material. In rush work baskets, thin splits of oak or palmetto butt are tied onto the preceding stitch. Mt. Pleasant sewers splice their strips of palm leaf by threading the pointed head of the new binder directly under the last stitch. They pull it through almost to the tail, then tuck the head of the old binder and the tail of the new binder between the rows, wrapping the whole bundle tightly before beginning the next stitch. Because the stitches do not interlock but are laid immediately next to the stitches of the preceding row, they radiate straight out from the center knot like the spokes of a wheel. Right-handed sewers coil the foundation grass clockwise around the center knot, so the binder slants backward; "left-handed baskets" are coiled counter-clockwise and the stitches slant forward.

Sometimes every stitch will pass through the foundation material of the adjacent row, but if a sewer is trying to work quickly, he or she will "wrap" the palm around the bundle every other stitch. The result is a slight loss of strength but a gain in speed of construction. So that the space between stitches will not become too wide as the circumference of the basket grows, the sewer periodically adds extra wrapped stitches. Certain Mt. Pleasant basketmakers, like Blanche Watts and Mary Jackson, have earned reputations for their flawless stitching and their attention to symmetry. Others specialize in extremely narrow rows and tight coils—Irene Foreman, Cathy Johnson, and Althea Coakley, to name a few.

To end a basket, Mt. Pleasant sewers cut the foundation grass on a long diagonal, stitch until the bundle tapers off, then backstitch a few inches. Janie Mazyck's technique on this storage basket is a rare example of a sewer backstitching the entire top row of a basket. Ms. Mazyck also made a fanner using this technique. The two baskets closely resemble the African storage and fanner baskets pictured in the chapter on basketry in John Michael

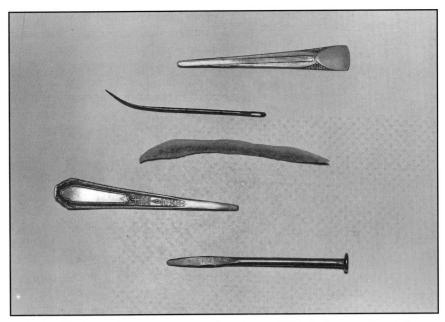

Sewing Bones: Teaspoon Handle (used as a teaching tool by Bea Coaxum), Bagging Needle (used by George Brown), Cow Rib (made by Sue Middleton), Teaspoon Handle (used by Florence Mazyck), Nail (used as a teaching tool by Mary Jackson).

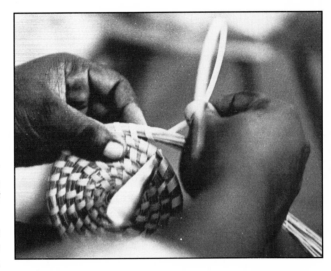

Steps in Sewing

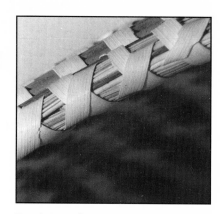

Detail: Rim of Storage Basket (Cat. 30)

Vlach's catalog, *The African American Tradition in Decorative Arts*, and may have been modeled on them.[14]

The strength of a basket depends on how firmly the stitches are pulled, as well as on which materials are used. Rush makes the stoutest basket; sweetgrass comes next. Very occasionally, Mt. Pleasant baskets are built entirely of longleaf pine straw, when a basketmaker "has a whim to make a 'pine' basket," or when sweetgrass is running short. Basketmakers acknowledge that pine straw baskets are softer and more likely to lose their shape when they dry out. Using pine needles in the coil also complicates the sewing process. Because they are short they have to be fed more frequently into the row, and because they are soft the stitches must be pulled especially tight.[15]

The choice of foundation material is determined most often by structural or aesthetic considerations, but there are times when chance plays a part. Describing a big "picnic" or "travelling" basket which Greg Day and Kate Young were buying for the Smithsonian, Mary Jane Manigault explained that she had sewn two rows of pine straw into the side of the basket because she was working at night, had run out of "rushes," and didn't want to go out to the barn to get more.[16]

Being more pliable, pine straw is easier than sweetgrass to tie into knots, either to start a coil or to embellish the outside of a row. "Pine knots" first appeared as a decorative device around 1950.[17] They are made by tying a small bundle of pine needles in one or more places. The bundle is then fed into the row as

the coil is sewn onto the basket. Individual sewers may group rows of pine straw in a distinctive pattern of "bands." This signature may be used in keeping accounts, to tell one person's work from another's when they show their baskets together.[18]

Pine straw and pine knots are worked into the row so that they will be clearly visible once the basket is finished. In a "played out" or flared form, a sewer will feed pine on the side of the row that faces up. In a "hauled in" or closed form, the outside is more highly decorated. If the designer wants pine to show on the cover of a basket the needles must be added to the "back" side of a row, that is, the side that faces down on the lap, since the cover will be inverted on the finished basket.

Basket covers may be flat, domed, steeple-shaped, or knob topped. Straight-sided cake baskets and semi-spherical sewing baskets traditionally were covered by flat lids. "Steeple top" is a new name for an old form.[19] It refers to the steep slope of the lid, and may have originated as a "pointed cover" superimposed on a sewing basket body. "Knob tops" or "top knots" protrude so that they can be grasped to remove the cover. Some knob tops are sewn with an opening, through which cord or yarn can be pulled without taking the lid off the basket. These last two cover types are combined in the cord basket, whose lid ascends sharply toward an open top knot.

On a straight-sided basket, the cover simply rests on the rim, but if the basket has a "lip," the sides of the cover may be drawn in slightly, making a snug fit. Covers also may be inset, or attached by hinges and latches. Hinges are constructed by closely wrapping a length of the foundation in one of the upper rows, then bringing it back into the basket body so that it forms a loop to the side. A similar loop is fashioned on the cover, passed through the loop on the basket base, and sewn back into the row of the cover. To make a latch, a loop is formed on the side of the basket base, as if for a hinge. On the cover, however, the wrapped grass is turned perpendicular to the plane of the top, forming a ring which can be inserted in the loop on the basket base.

Side handles are made by reinforcing the bundle with additional grass and dividing it into two parts. One part is stitched to the basket body; the other is wrapped and extended out to the side, where it rejoins the row a few inches around the basket.

On old-style baskets, side handles consist of a single row, wrapped closely so that the binder entirely conceals the foundation

Cookie Jar Basket

material. Modern basketmakers generally sew a second row onto the first to strengthen the handle. Openwork borders are made by a similar procedure: the top row or two are detached from the basket body, then brought back and stitched in place at regular intervals. Lately, sewers have added a new twist to openwork, twining two or more wrapped rows around each other and stitching them to the rim, giving the effect of a rope.

Cross-handles commonly extend from the basket rim and may be as wide as five rows, stitched together for strength. Sea Island sewers have used materials other than grass to make handles. At the Penn School, basketry students learned to lash a rigid splint handle onto the sides of a coiled basket, passing it first through a row near the top.[20] Allen Green, on Sapelo Island, makes a short, looped handle from a strip of palmetto stem which he doubles back, twists, and attaches to the cover of his sewing basket.

Among Mt. Pleasant basketmakers, Mary Jane Manigault is known for her "ring of handles,"[21] a technique sewers have adapted to anchor strap handles on plant hanger baskets. As an example of a double, hinged cross-handle, Irene Foreman's pail-shaped basket is one-of-a-kind. Many contemporary sewers attach cross-handles by bringing a secondary coil around the basket body and then carrying it over the top. Mary Jackson's "two-lips basket" is an exceptionally artful variation of this traditional technique.

As surface decorations, secondary coils are recent features on Mt. Pleasant baskets, dating perhaps from the 1960s. A bundle of pine straw, sweetgrass or, occasionally, rush is sewn on the outside of a basket, either by tying into the foundation material or by passing a stitch under the palm of the underlying row. To create a pleasing effect, a sewer may attach a secondary coil in angular or looped patterns on the sides of the basket, or embellish a top knot with "fins" or "ridges."[22]

Basketmakers who consistently produce new or "own style" designs are esteemed in their community as masters of the art. Not surprisingly, sewers jealously guard their inventions. Originality usually consists of combining parts of old forms in new ways, or changing the size of individual parts in relation to each other.[23] Thus, a new-style basket may combine the traditional body shape of a sewing basket, the conical cover of a cord basket, and the high cross-handle of a flower tray. An important motive for innovation is that "different looking baskets" sell fast.

Yet, as in all traditional crafts, the best guarded innovations do not stay secret for long. Changes in styles and in the use of materials are invariably studied, imitated, and rejected or adopted by the community of sewers at large. Far from discouraging experimentation and originality the basketmaking community disperses new shapes and techniques, so that they become collective property, belonging to many or all.

Basketmaking in Mt. Pleasant tends to be a family enterprise. Husbands, fathers, and brothers gather sweetgrass, rush, and palmetto, offering the materials first to their women folk and selling the surplus to other basketmakers in the community. Mothers, daughters, and sisters often market their baskets together, taking turns selling, or assigning the job to one family member. It is not uncommon for a basket to include the work of more than one person. Experienced sewers often build upon bottoms made by children in their families. A basketmaker might buy a number of bottoms from another sewer, to increase the speed of production. In some families the division of labor may be clear-cut, and take on the character of a cottage industry, with the least experienced sewers making bottoms, the more skillful building up the sides, and the most proficient doing "finish" work.

Mt. Pleasant sewers typically begin to learn the craft at the age of six or seven. Their teachers may be their mothers, grandmothers, great-aunts, or great-grandmothers, depending on who is caring for the children and has the time to make baskets and teach. Boys learn to sew along with girls and, though few boys stick with it beyond adolescence, some men return to basketmaking when they leave the work force.

A group of children living in a family settlement might gather around an older kinswoman, who will start the knot and stitch the first row or two for each youngster. "Then we just sew till we got a certain size," relates Helen Gadsden, "and she'd start another one and we'd go on and on and on until we'd get perfect on what we're doing and get on making our own baskets."[24] Children learn mainly by watching their elders and sometimes are spurred by competition with their peers. At the end of the day, young sewers might compare their work to see whose baskets are the neatest and who has accomplished the most. They may be required to sew a certain number of "bottoms," which they are paid for or encouraged to sell on the family basket stand. This was even more common when

Hinge; High-Handled Covered Basket (Cat. 23)

Twisted Rim: Casserole Holder (Cat. 46)

Side-Handle: 19th Century Sewing Basket

Cross-Handle: Sewing Basket (Cat. 13)

Cross-Handle: Flower Basket

15

Sewing Basket (Cat. 31)

Sewing Basket by Mary Jane Manigault, 1971

the middle generation of sewers was young. "We had to do that. It was a must," one basketmaker says, recalling her great-grandmother's rule that each child sew two trivets before bedtime. "It seemed hard at the time but she was trying to help us learn how to get things for ourselves."[25] Mae Bell Coakley remembers the children in her family having their own little stand "around side of momma's stand. We would get so excited when someone stopped."[26]

Children initially learn how to make the knot, begin the coil, feed in grass, insert new strips of palmetto, and "end off" the basket. Once a beginner masters these basic steps, he or she practices "turning up" a basket. A young sewer generally starts with a round bread tray, considered the easiest shape to make. Some ambitious beginners attempt complex shapes right away. Carlton Rouse's flower basket, for example, is one of the first styles he learned to sew, with help and encouragement from his aunt, Mary Vanderhorst.

Gradually, the apprentice tries more advanced techniques: adding pine straw for color; playing out and hauling in the sides of a basket; making covers; attaching side handles and cross-handles; sewing openwork borders, secondary coils, hinges, latches, and feet. Only accomplished sewers undertake the most difficult traditional forms—ring trays, hat box baskets, and missionary bags.

Learning is a matter of imitation. Yet basketmakers who stay with the craft continually re-shape its rules in their own ways. Not only every individual, but every generation makes a different style of baskets.[27] Today sewers enjoy unprecedented freedom of design, creating fanciful shapes like milk jugs, pitchers, cups and saucers, bells, and intricate openwork wall mats. Some basketmakers bend the grasses into "broken corners" and six- and eight-sided baskets, turning angles and mastering forms undreamed of in the past.

The Mt. Pleasant baskets chosen for this exhibition range from the first attempts of a five-year-old to the mature work of a life-long basketmaker. Several baskets represent different generations of a single family—in one case four generations are represented. Some of the baskets were sewn by men. For ten years Jessie Bennett had been producing bottoms and placemats and helping market the family's work before "raising" his first basket—a large, round, straight-sided market basket of sweetgrass, rush, and pine. His wife Mary Jane finished the top row and added a cross-handle, reinforcing it with a secondary coil of rush. Because Jessie is right-handed and Mary left-handed, their work is easily distinguished.

Joseph Foreman was using an old-style cake basket he had made for holding change at his new vegetable stand, where he also displays baskets sewn by family members and neighbors. He agreed to sell his basket, protesting quietly that basketmaking is "on the woman's side."[28] He learned to make baskets as a boy, growing up in a family of renowned sewers. Mr. Foreman's cake basket, shallow enough to be held in one hand, closely resembles those made in the early 1900s. His wife Evelyina also comes from a line of famous basketmakers—the Manigaults. Mrs. Foreman's sewing basket is a variation of an old style, with straighter sides and a hinged cover. The Foremans' daughters are adept at both traditional baskets and new designs. Yvonne Foreman's hat box basket is a splendid rendition of an old form, embellished with pine knots. Her sister, Mary Jackson, radically reinterpreted the traditional sewing basket, using all three foundation materials in quick succession, and shaping the basket wide and low. For the cover she began with pine, intro-

Carlton Rouse Holding His Flower Basket (Cat. 47)

Detail: Left- and Right-Handed Sewing, Market Basket (Cat. 52)

Three Difficult Traditional Forms: Hat Box, Missionary Bag, Ring Tray (Cat. 38, 28, 24)

duced sweetgrass right away on the inside of the coil, and inserted a row of pine knots on what would be the outside, before switching to rush. This new sewing basket has the look of thrown pottery, taut, dark, and polished.

Contemporary basketmakers draw inspiration from everyday objects. Distinguished among the new-style baskets on exhibit is Sue Middleton's flower vase, with its "broken

Sewing Basket (Cat. 37)

corners" and solid footing. Beginning with a round bottom, this basket plays out into a bulbous, four-sided urn—a great feat of construction. Mrs. Middleton interpreted the shape from something she saw on television, its classical lines notwithstanding.

Marie Manigault's footed cake tray, based on a commercial "cake house," and Florence Mazyck's openwork basket, copying a clothes hamper she saw at K-Mart, show how basketmakers recreate the commonplace in coiled grass. The importance of African forms is not confined to the past; Africa continues to provide models today. Helen Gadsden's version of a traditional cord basket, with its steep conical lid, for example, was derived from an illustration in a book on African household objects. Because the basket appears exotic, one might guess it is an old style, but it has only recently appeared in Mt. Pleasant.

The Rice Kingdom

African American sea grass basketry has evolved, over three hundred years, from an agricultural and household craft practiced primarily in the slave quarters of lowcountry plantations, to a modern art form produced for sale. The first basketmakers most likely came from rice-growing areas of Africa. Lowcountry rice planters preferred to buy slaves from regions where people knew how to cultivate and "clean" the grain, where rice was a staple of the diet.[29] In Africa, basketry was not a specialized trade. Fences, gra-

naries, reed work, thatching, traps, and heavy field baskets tended to be made by the men who used them; mats, smaller baskets for storing and serving food, and fancy baskets were made by women for their own households.[30] Though coiled baskets appear everywhere in Africa, lowcountry baskets are related most closely to those made by the Senegambian, Angolan, and Congolese peoples of the Atlantic coast.[31]

To the extent that the lowcountry plantation was a little world unto itself, it was supported by the work of numerous slave artisans—carpenters, coopers, blacksmiths, brickmakers, masons, potters, seamstresses, and basketmakers—who produced goods and provided services more cheaply than they could be bought. Although basketmaking was regarded as a seasonal farm chore and did not have the status of other artisan trades, basketmaking skills increased the value of a slave. A man or woman who made baskets was worth more than one who did not, age, strength, and other skills being equal.[32]

On some plantations, slaves made baskets not only for use on the premises but for sale to other plantations. This practice occurred at least as early as the Revolutionary period, when one William Gibbons, a Savannah River rice planter, listed in his Account Book in 1774, various amounts "pade for baskets," ranging from 3 shillings to 8 pounds 9 shillings—a high figure, even considering the inflated value of the colonial currency.[33] Baskets were exchanged in cross-plantation trade up until the Civil War. Allen Green, a Sapelo Island basketmaker, reports that his grandfather, Allen Smith, worked on a plantation near Macon, Georgia, making baskets for his master to sell: "He make baskets and 'e marster sell it from one plantation to the next plantation. That was his job."[34]

Besides making baskets for their masters, some plantation hands practiced the craft in their free time, for their own purposes. On rice plantations, under the prevailing organization of labor known as the "task" system, slaves worked as individuals, not in gangs as in most of the South. Once a worker finished his daily "task"—a standardized quantity of work, such as hoeing a quarter-acre—the rest of the day was his, or hers. Workers commonly used the time to cultivate small garden crops, to raise hogs and poultry, or to make boats, nets, brooms, and baskets—all items with a ready market. They also might make things for personal use.[35] On May 3, 1851, for instance, Thomas B. Chaplin, a St. Helena Is-

Open Work Hamper (Cat. 44)

land cotton planter, caught his slave Jim "plaiting a palmetto hat, setting up in bed," when he was supposed to be lying down sick.[36]

Basketmaking was at times assigned to slaves who were no longer fit for fieldwork. In March, 1846, Chaplin "put old May to making baskets, 2 a week"[37]—though what kind of baskets Chaplin does not say. References to basketry in old documents rarely identify the type. Plaited palmetto, coiled grass, and splintwork baskets all were made on lowcountry plantations. On Argyle Plantation, in the Savannah River basin, for example, the overseer reported two hands "cutting oak for baskets" one year, and four hands "sent for rushes" another year.[38] Heavy, durable split oak baskets were used to harvest cotton and provision crops like corn and potatoes. Open splintwork, such as sieves, drying trays, and fish traps, served special functions. Coiled baskets, more flexible and closely woven, were ideal for winnowing and storing grain.

The same workers may have made several types of baskets; basketmakers who sewed coiled baskets with white oak weavers had to know how to split oak. Allen Smith, for one, made "all class of baskets"—coiled grass fanners, plaited palmetto forms, and various sizes of split oak containers. Allen Green reports, "he make rice fanner, quart, peck, half-a-peck—didn't have no scale—made quart, bushel basket. He made all class."[39]

Basketmaking is usually reported to have been men's work on lowcountry plantations. "There were men on the places who were good handicraftsmen," wrote David Doar, recalling plantation life on the Santee River before the Civil War. "They made all the baskets (out of river rushes cured and sewed with white oak strips) that were used on the place."[40] Collecting materials might occupy a few hands for several days, usually late in the summer; making baskets might take two or three weeks, just before the crop was harvested. "Jacob and Jim getting stuff for baskets,"[41] a Berkeley County planter wrote—and indexed—in his Journal on August 27, 1836. "Jacob was occupied 3 weeks in making baskets."[42] Similarly, the hands "sent for rushes" on Argyle Plantation in August, 1830, spent three days at the task. The next year, the overseer needed more baskets—perhaps the rice crop looked exceptionally good—and for two weeks in August he assigned two workers to "making baskets."

There is evidence that women also were capable basketmakers. Elizabeth Allston Pringle, of Georgetown County, told of an outstanding weaver named Maria, who came

Santee River Fanner and Small Round Basket (Cat. 2, 9)

from royalty in Africa. She had been taken in battle by an enemy tribe, and sold to a slaveship with her kinsmen Tom and Prince. "Maum Maria made wonderful baskets and wove beautiful rugs from the rushes that grew along Long Cane Creek," Pringle wrote in *Chronicles of Chicora Wood.* These "three quite remarkable, tall, fine-looking, and very intelligent Africans . . . occupied an important place in my mother's recollections of early childhood."[43] Adele Petigru Allston, Mrs. Pringle's mother, was unusual in the antebellum period for valuing the beauty of her slaves' handcrafts. When it came to appreciating what slaves did with their time, most planters cared only for utility.

Once the rice was threshed and ready for pounding and winnowing, dozens of fanner baskets would be issued. On Argyle Plantation, for example, beginning in November, as many as fifty-three hands were engaged in "thrashing and winnowing rice." These workers appear only as numbers on the daily entry, but are listed by name under the heading "Disbursement of tools and baskets," at the end of the overseer's report.

To date, the earliest documentation of fanner baskets in South Carolina is found in a Charleston County register of wills and inventories. Fanners were listed among the personal effects of Noah Serre on May 18, 1730, and of Joseph Wilkinson on June 10, 1745.[44] The oldest artifact of actual basketry is a fragment dating from the Revolutionary period

"The Threshing Floor," Watercolor by Alice R. H. Smith

18th Century Basket Fragment

until after the Revolutionary War.[49] Yet on every plantation, workers continued to pound rice by hand—"a very hard and severe operation," wrote Alexander Garden in 1755, "as each Slave is tasked at Seven Mortars for One Day and each Mortar Contains three pecks of Rice."[50]

The first successful pounding mill was built by Jonathan Lucas in 1787 at Peachtree Plantation on the Santee River. It was powered by water released from a reservoir. Within four years, "Lucas had developed a tide-powered mill and, by 1817, one driven by steam." Pounding mills marked a great advance in rice production and, while their impact was not of the same magnitude, they had "virtually the same significance for the rice kingdom as Eli Whitney's gin for cotton."[51] Around 1811, a threshing mill was devised, "and the prosperous era of the grain began."[52]

Winnowing houses took over the function of separating the chaff from the grain. Raised on posts about fifteen feet high, these simple structures had a grating in the floor through which the threshed and pounded seed was dropped. Precisely when winnowing houses were introduced has not been determined, but by 1800 they were in operation on virtually all rice plantations.[53] As the century progressed, the winnowing process was further mechanized in some mills with the installation of screens and wind fans.[54]

Still, old methods persisted alongside the new. Rarely does one see a drawing or photograph of a winnowing house without noticing a basket somewhere. In the slave quarters, families continued to use fanners to "clean" the rough rice which was issued to them as rations or rewards, or which they grew for themselves on individual plots.[55] Besides working rice, fanners were used for winnowing "benne" and sorghum seed, for "raking grits," and for carrying husked corn, peas, and other produce too small to be contained in a splintwork basket. "Boys and girls would come in procession with their 'fanners' filled with corn perched on the top of their heads," reported a northern teacher stationed at Beaufort during the Civil War. "Singing and laughing and joking they would wait for hours for a turn to grind."[56]

Fanners served some unexpected functions as well. Alice Ravenel Huger Smith's watercolor of "The Plantation Street" on a Carolina rice plantation of the 1850s shows Negro babies "sunning in blanket-padded 'fanner baskets,' supervised by a 'mauma,' or nurse"— an image Smith's father recalled vividly from

which was excavated recently from the bottom of a privy at the Heyward-Washington House in Charleston.[45] As more waterlogged sites are studied, even older examples of both basketry and textiles likely will be found.[46] Although no seventeenth century evidence has turned up yet, it is logical to assume that fanner baskets were used to process the first crops of rice grown in Carolina, possibly as early as 1672.

Planters soon began experimenting with machines to replace ancient African hand techniques and to overcome the "incredible difficulties in preparing, or dressing, the rice for market."[47] In 1691, Peter Jacob Guerard patented "a Pendulum Engine," hoping to improve upon the mortar and pestle. Though reputed to perform "much better and in lesse time and labour huske rice" than any other device, Guerard's invention did not catch on.[48] A "pecker" machine worked by oxen was used

"Rice Culture on the Ogeechee, Near Savannah, Georgia" from *Harper's Weekly*, January 5, 1867

his youth on a Combahee River rice plantation. "On fine days," he wrote, "there might be seen on the open ground" in front of the sickhouse, which doubled as a nursery," a large number of 'fanner-baskets,' and on each basket a folded blanket, and on each blanket a baby."[57]

The repertory of coiled baskets in the antebellum period included not only large work and storage baskets, but also a "wider range of domestic items."[58] One household basket, described in detail by David Doar, demonstrates an African design principle. Plantation craftsmen, Doar wrote, made "a very neat sewing basket" using "a finer kind of grass, sewed with palmetto or oak strip." Some sewing baskets were "three-storied, that is, one on top of the other, each resting on the cover of the one below and getting smaller as they went up."[59] Both "double" and "triple" baskets, stacked vertically, "with each succeeding volume sewn into the lid of the preceding one," are found in the repertory of Mt. Pleasant sewers. Greg Day cites the form as an example of the African "additive approach to design," a linear repetition of units which also shows up in the African American strip quilt. Simi-

Winnowing House, 19th Century

21

"Plantation Street," Watercolor by Alice R. H. Smith

Double Basket (Cat. 50)

larly, the twentieth-century "in-and-out" design repeats, in vertical tiers, the shape of an older form, the cord basket.[60]

The "head tote basket" was essentially a deep version of the fanner. It, too, was distinctly African, and it outlasted the plantation era. Native Americans typically carried heavy loads in "burden baskets" strapped to their backs by a "tump line" across the forehead; European-Americans lifted their splintwork harvest and market baskets by means of side handles extending from the rim or a cross-handle made from a stout central rib. In contrast, African Americans continued the practice of bearing loads on the head, "in the manner of their African ancestors."[61]

Unlike oak, sea grass does not lend itself to the fabrication of handles strong enough to support great weights. Coiled cross-handles began appearing only after 1900, and then only on sweetgrass baskets. A unique hybrid form made on St. Helena Island—an oblong rush basket with a wood strap handle lashed onto the sides—suggests even more clearly a borrowing from splintwork traditions.

Outside influences may also be traced to European wickerware, imported principally from Germany at the end of the nineteenth century. "Basketmaking in Europe was at its high point," remarks Jeanette Lasansky, an expert on Pennsylvania basket traditions.[62] Willow baskets, with their intricately woven rims, feet, and handles, and their great variety of forms, were especially popular. By the early 1900s, some of these imports may have suggested new ideas to African American basketmakers. Coiled bread baskets, for example, are said to derive from wickerware serving trays. The first missionary bags may have been modeled on the purses in which Quaker missionaries carried their Bibles.[63] Coiled flower baskets follow the lines of large, flat Victorian "provender" baskets. "Wall pockets" were familiar fancywork projects for Victorian ladies.[64] Lowcountry sewers adapted the form to sweetgrass, attaching conical and cylindrical containers to flat backs which could be hung on the wall.

While openwork borders, feet, handles, and even the shapes of some baskets may have been inspired by European-derived examples, the true mother of invention was necessity. When resources are limited, people turn to materials at hand and use their ingenuity. Recalling a basket her great-grandmother wove from honeysuckle vines, a Mt. Pleasant sewer recently declared, "there's a lot of things God created in this world that we could use, but it just takes a little mind and time to do it."[65]

A heroic case in point is related in the narrative of Jack Frowers, a South Carolina field hand interviewed in 1864 by a journalist at the Federal army camp in Beaufort, South Carolina.[66] Seeking freedom, Frowers created a coiled grass boat to carry him to Union-held territory at Port Royal. On the first of June, according to an eyewitness account, "there came into our lines . . . a short, stout, thickset negro man," about 45 years of age, who "landed from a primitive boat, not made of bulrushes, but from a coarse kind of grass, which had first been twisted into a rope an inch and a half in diameter. To keep this rope together, it was bound round, or, as the sailors would term it, 'served' with other grass."

The Yankee newsman closely observed the sewing technique and plan of Frowers' boat. The rope, he reported, "was plaited together, as I have seen doormats, beginning in the centre, and building out to form the foundation, or floor, then up to form the sides." What he describes is an immense coiled basket—"five feet four inches in length, three feet four inches broad, and one foot six inches in depth." Fastened to the floor of the boat, "to keep it from collapsing, there were three pieces of pine wood." On the bottom was nailed an old shutter, perhaps as a keel. "Inside and outside," the boat "was pitched, to keep it water tight."

In construction, the vessel recalls African and Native American antecedents; in spirit it brings to mind the Biblical story of Moses. This last association would have been familiar to lowcountry Negroes. Current among slaves on the Combahee River, for example, in the years before the War, was a religious song chanted at "shoutings." D. E. Huger Smith recorded two verses in *A Charlestonian's Recollections*, including the lines: "Moses in de bull-rushes fas' asleep!/ Playing possum in de two bushel basket!"

Frowers, in his report to the journalist, was intent on describing technique. "I got an axe and knife—no matter how—and I cut a lot of rushes, and went to work in the wood and made this boat." He spent two days weaving it "after the stuff was all ready." He got pitch "by cutting into a tree and catching the gum." The old shutter came from the house of his recent master, Dr. Henry Fuller. When Frowers finished his work, he hid out another day, and then paddled to Port Royal, "too glad to get away."

Triple-Decker Yarn Basket (Cat. 49)

Women Vendors, Near the Citadel, Charleston, South Carolina, 1895

Wall Pocket (Cat. 25)

Planting Sweet Potatoes, James Hopkinson's Plantation, Edisto Island, South Carolina, 1862

Frowers' basketmaking skills served him well in a moment of desperate opportunity. When the Sea Islands fell to the Union Army, blacks from all over the lowcountry fled to freedom. After the War this movement of people continued, and the tradition of coiled basketry moved with them. Frances Jones, known affectionately as the "Daufuskie Mayor," traces her basketmaking ability to her "great-great-great grandfather," Frederick Locks, who was born a slave on St. Simons Island, Georgia, and near the end of the War came by boat to Hilton Head, later settling with his family on Daufuskie.[67]

Allen Green's grandfather, Allen Smith, brought with him the basketmaking skills he had practiced inland, when he and his family migrated to Sapelo Island sometime after 1865. As an old man, Smith was still making baskets, no longer for a plantation master but for the new "master" of Sapelo. Having acquired the Island in 1912, Howard Coffin, from Detroit, Michigan, bought all the baskets Smith was willing to sell, for ten and fifteen cents apiece.[68]

Family Farms and City Markets

At the end of the War, plantation facilities lay in ruins, the labor force had been emancipated, and many landowners lacked the capital to start planting again. Competition from new plantation economies in Southeast Asia, and from large, efficient rice tracts in Louisiana and Texas had begun to undermine the agricultural price structure even before 1860.[69] The success of growers in the old Southwest, whom the War had passed over lightly, made rice in South Carolina a poor investment. When cultivation resumed it was on a new basis. Plantations frequently were leased or run by managers employed by absentee landlords. The work was done by free men and women for wages, for a share of the crop, or for land. Under a contractual arrangement called the "two-day system," workers exchanged labor for a few acres of land, plus living quarters and fuel.

Despite valiant efforts to revive rice production, the plantations never recovered. Rice operations which had managed to struggle past 1890 were dealt fatal blows by hurricanes that ripped the shoreline, inundated islands, and flooded low-lying fields in 1893, 1894, 1898, 1906, 1910, 1911, and 1916.

What did these events and trends mean for the craft of coiled basketry? With the break-up of the plantation system, many blacks acquired land and began to farm for themselves on a small scale. In essence, a class of black landowners emerged in the lowcountry, rather than the sharecroppers and tenant farmers who typified other parts of the South. Many of these independent people would work seasonally on nearby plantations, but most also raised gardens and sold produce of their own. Coiled grass baskets, including fanners, remained in use in their homes and fields.

The free black community of Mt. Pleasant dates from the 1870s. Today's older generation grew up on farms belonging to their parents and grandparents, farms ranging in size from ten to fifty acres.[70] Half the acreage usually was planted in cotton; the other half was planted in foodstuffs—rice, corn, sweet potatoes, millet, and a variety of summer vegetables. Cotton, the mainstay of the agrarian economy until World War II, brought cash only once a year—if then. After deductions were made for food and for

Work Baskets on Sandy Island, ca. 1930. Photograph by Bayard Wooten

items advanced to the farmer during the year, what cash was left over might be paid to him in scrip—a currency made of paper, metal, or even wood, that was redeemable only in local commissaries.

But black farmers who owned land and produced a surplus of food products could enter the market economy directly. Fanners and vegetable baskets became a familiar sight on the streets of Charleston. African Americans from communities near the city, such as James Island, Johns Island, Edisto Island, and Mt. Pleasant, rode the ferries to Charleston, toting vegetables, flowers, pelts, fishing nets, and fish and shellfish gathered from the tidal creeks. Seafood was carried to market in sacks or in split oak baskets with handles; vegetables were transported as a rule in coiled rush baskets balanced on the head.

So striking was this phenomenon that a minor genre of street vendor photography emerged, notably in the work of George W. Johnson. "One of the most interesting sights of Charleston," touted the caption of a turn-of-the-century postcard, "is the negro vegetable vendor." On the streets of the city, visitors could see vendors "of both sexes and of all ages . . . bearing on their heads enormous round baskets of produce," and hear them "singing their wares in quaint dialect cries that sound to the unfamiliar ear like utterances of a foreign race."[71] At a time when wealthy Americans were discovering the pleasures of watering holes in the Caribbean and pueblos in the Spanish Southwest, Charleston promoters were making the point that their city had exotic people, too.

Not everyone was happy with this image. When the South Carolina Inter-State and West Indian Exposition of 1901 unveiled a sculpture in front of the "Negro Building," educated blacks protested that the work represented "the Negro in a too menial guise." The crowning symbol of this romantic statue was a black woman, her chin held high, balancing a basket on top of her head. The basket itself was a mixed image of two craft traditions—shaped like a coiled vegetable basket, its texture appears to be that of splintwork. The "Negro Group" was in the same mode as late-nineteenth century European sculptures which celebrated the heroic peasant. Below the woman stands a bare-chested blacksmith resting on an anvil, and to his left sits a boy playing a banjo. "No sooner was the group in place in the beautiful grove of oaks which shelters the Negro building," reported the monthly newsletter of the Exposition, "when it created

quite a commotion among the so-called 'new' negroes of Charleston."[72] The blacks' protest was a partial success: the sculpture was moved to another site on the Exposition grounds, in the Court of Palaces, where it was duly photographed by G. W. Johnson.

Savannah, like Charleston, had been a major exporter of rice, and by 1900 served as an outlet for the small surpluses harvested by black farmers and fishermen. As recently as 1940, baskets were in daily use in city neighborhoods and outlying communities. Researchers for the Georgia Writers' Project discovered several men, and one woman, in the Savannah area, still making coiled baskets in the late 1930s. The fieldworkers published their findings in a superb compilation of oral history, *Drums and Shadows: Survival Studies Among the Georgia Coastal Negroes.* Near Old

Abraham Herriott Pounding Rice on Sandy Island, South Carolina, ca. 1930

The "Negro Group" at the Inter-State and West Indian Exposition. Photograph by G. W. Johnson

Young James Islanders. Photograph by G. W. Johnson

Vegetable Woman. Photograph by G. W. Johnson

Street Vendors, 1876. Copyrighted by Kilburn Brothers

Fort, an African American community in the extreme northeastern section of Savannah, they had interviewed "a Negro basketmaker" by the name of John Haynes, who declared he was "carrying on the tradition of his ancestors." He said that for generations, the men of his family had passed on the crafts of woodcarving, basketmaking, and "various phases of weaving." Haynes only made baskets, both bullrush bound with scrub palmetto, "of the coil type," and plaited white oak splintwork. His stock and trade included "hampers, flat clothes baskets, farm and shopping baskets, and the popular 'fanner' which the Negro vendors balance gracefully on their heads as they walk about the city, displaying a colorful array of merchandise."[73]

Before and after emancipation, Savannah was the market town for blacks who lived on the South Carolina Sea Islands nearest to Georgia. Caesar Johnson, born in 1872, was perhaps the best known basketmaker on Hilton Head. "Corn, sweet potatoes, peas, melons, tomatoes—we take 'em to the ol' time ma'aket in Sabannah," he told a reporter for *The Savannah News*, in a 1960 interview.[74] "He tore down now, the Ma-aket," he observed. Johnson mourned its passing and worried about the Negroes who still were trying to make a living "in de old way." He recalled the trip to Savannah by ferry and steamer, and the stops along the route. Besides garden produce, he used to carry fish, oysters, strings of dried mullet, and baskets, too, for sale in the city. He remembered one basket customer in particular. "Jedge Saussey, (the late Judge Gordon Saussy) he buy two of de big baskets I make. He 'gage me most particular, 'case he want to show he little chillun how t'ings used to be in ol' days gone by." Nowadays, Johnson lamented, you "couldn't sell four crates of beans" along St. Julian Street.

"Native Island Basketry" on St. Helena

Early in the Civil War, as part of the Federal occupation of Port Royal, northern missionaries, philanthropists, and soldiers launched a bold experiment to "test the capabilities of the Negro for freedom and self-support and self-improvement."[75] At the center of the experiment was the Penn School, on St. Helena Island, an abolitionist enterprise initially supported

Baskets by Ceasar Johnson (Cat. 7, 14)

by northern relief agencies. While in general, northern interest in the Sea Island Negro waned rapidly after the War, the Penn School endured. By 1890, independent black farmers had established themselves solidly in Beaufort County. The Penn School was their chief educational resource.

Between 1900 and 1904, Penn was reorganized after the "industrial" pattern of Hampton Institute in Virginia. A new board of trustees, headed by Dr. Hollis Burke Frissell, Hampton's Principal, and financed from the North, began another "experiment."[76] Penn's name was changed to Penn Normal, Industrial, and Agricultural School. The "Industrial" in its title referred to manual training in trades and crafts. It had nothing to do with preparing people for urban factory jobs. In fact, the School's avowed aim was to keep people on the land. How could Penn hope to arm them against the temptation to leave? By "assuring them of economic independence and dignified living in their rural communities."[77]

Basketry Class of Alfred Graham, 1905

27

Alfred Graham in 1909. Photograph by Leigh Richmond Miner

The Penn School's new curriculum was organized into Industrial Departments for boys, Domestic Science for girls, and Academic and Agricultural Departments for both. Manual arts originally included basketry, carpentry, and cobbling. Soon, harnessmaking, blacksmithing, and wheelwrighting joined the list of trades.

When Rossa Belle Cooley arrived on St. Helena in 1905 to become Principal of the Penn School, she found only one native domestic craft still practiced—"the making of baskets similar to those found in some parts of Africa today, artistic and durable, soft brown in color." She was puzzled to discover that basketry was men's work. "Why don't the women make baskets?" she asked. Cooley organized a group of women—eleven girls were enrolled in the class that year, along with thirty-eight boys—and "invited the old basketmaker to come in and give them pointers." At first all went well. "Off we started and they were a happy, busy, picturesque crowd." Yet something seemed amiss. Although the girls finished their work, "they did not rejoice in their baskets." Years later, Cooley learned from a missionary who was visiting the School "that women do not make baskets in Africa! And so," she concluded,

trusting this doubtful premise, "women don't make baskets on St. Helena." It was a man's craft and would remain so, she surmised, "until the race changes by many more decades of contact with a new environment."[78] After this initial co-educational trial, girls rarely were assigned to the basketry shop.

The first basketmaking instructor at Penn was Alfred Graham, a native islander, who had "learned the art from his African father."[79] Graham lived at Indian Hill Plantation, in a "double-pen" cabin immortalized in a 1909 photograph by Leigh Richmond Miner.[80] Graham is sitting on a chair in front of his home, sewing a basket bottom. To his right lie bundles of rush and palmetto weavers; to his left a child is seated on the ground, holding an oblong basket with a rigid strap handle. In the background, behind an immense yucca plant, rests a two-wheeled cart, and beyond that, Graham's wife sits quietly working on the porch of their cabin. The photograph of Graham first appeared in Penn School's *Annual Report* for 1910, above the caption, "The Basket Maker at Home." Another Miner photograph, published the year before, shows five different forms produced by the Basketry Department: a fanner, hung from a palmetto strip looped at the rim; scrap baskets in two sizes with wrapped side handles; a large, covered clothes hamper with wrapped side handles; a covered, oblong basket with a wooden cross-handle; and an oblong basket with inward sloping sides, used to hold firewood.

Penn's *Annual Reports* showed records of the enrollment, expenses, and income of all the School's departments. From year to year the *Reports* commented on the historical significance of "Native Island Basketry." "This industry was brought from Africa in the early slave days," declared the *Report* of 1910. It belongs "as truly to the Negro as the Indian basket belongs to the Indian." Describing Penn's program, the *Report* explained how rushes gathered from tidal rivers were "brought to the school shop in the Island bateaus." Palmetto stems were "stripped" to make the "thread" with which the baskets were sewn.

Penn's administrators perennially underscored the need to preserve coiled basketry. "This is the only real Negro craft inherited from African forefathers," the 1930 *Report* asserted, "and is so beautiful it seems important to preserve it. These baskets were useful in the field in plantation days and have been adapted for home use." Penn's northern supporters had a similar view. They regarded sea

Penn School Baskets. Photograph by Leigh Richmond Miner

grass baskets, like spirituals, as demonstrations of the artistic instincts of the Negro and a valuable heritage from his African past.[81]

Instruction in basketry also had a practical function: it gave "hand and eye training . . . to a group of boys."[82] Here was the celebrated rationale for industrial education, developed at Hampton Institute, where Rossa Cooley had worked for seven years before coming to St. Helena. Penn's curriculum would foster industry, precision, and persistence[83] while teaching trades "to help a rural community hold its boys."[84]

The School's promotion of coiled basketry spanned the eras of the arts-and-crafts movement at the turn of the century, the rural handicraft revival of the Depression years, and the rise of black nationalism in the 1920s and '30s. From all of these developments, the basketry program drew philosophical support. But from the start, its purposes were primarily economic. "There is a real commercial demand for these native island baskets," noted the *Annual Report* of 1910. For the following thirty-five years, Penn sold baskets made in the School's shop and in homes across St. Helena. From community people, Penn bought baskets outright, paying "cash direct to the basketmakers," after deducting ten percent of the selling price for handling. Local farm families used the income from baskets to help pay their property taxes.[85] The baskets Penn purchased in a given year sometimes exceeded sales, but whatever money the School earned was shown in accounts as offsetting the expenses of running the Department.

Basketry at Penn got off to a big start. Thirty-three boys were enrolled in the Department in 1904-5, the first year after the School's reorganization. By 1909-10, enrollment had risen to seventy-one—the largest number ever reported. The following year, Penn dedicated its Cope Industrial Building. It housed a new basketry shop which, it was hoped, would "make a larger output possible." In 1912-13, seventy baskets were sold, through either mail orders or retail outlets, bringing in $139.72. Sales increased the next year to a hundred baskets, earning $151.13. A "Trade Mark" tag, illustrated with a close-up of Alfred Graham taken from Miner's photograph, was attached to every basket shipped. By 1913, three arts and crafts shops—in Charleston, Philadelphia, and Boston—were carrying St. Helena baskets.[86]

In 1914, Franklin Capers replaced Graham as instructor of basketry. Fifty-three boys were enrolled in the class, and baskets were made

A "Daltha" Farmer Grinding Grain. Photograph by Leigh Richmond Miner

regularly in seven homes for sale to the School. Capers taught basketmaking for two years, at a salary of $210 and $127. In 1915-16, George Brown, a grandnephew of Alfred Graham and a graduate of Penn who had worked as a Farm Assistant for the School, took over the Basketry Department. Brown would teach basketmaking for the next thirty-four years, until Penn relinquished its role as a school and became a community center. His son, Leroy E. Browne, remembers him as a man with good eyes and incredibly strong hands. He had the whole Island at his disposal, says the younger Browne, to roam in search of materials. He would spend entire days, travelling by horse and buggy from one end of St. Helena to another. From the woods, he would take fronds from saw palmetto plants, preferring the tall ones—five and a half feet or more—so that once the stems were stripped into "threads" he wouldn't have to join them so often. He would cut palmetto in cooler seasons, fall or early spring; submerged in a tank of water, the strips would keep for months.[87]

Of two kinds of rush available on the Island, Leroy Browne explains, the fresh water variety was easy to find but too brittle to use for baskets. His father sought out the tall, green, salt water rush, which he harvested with a "marsh" or "reef" hook. He would "sift" a bundle, holding the rush upright in one

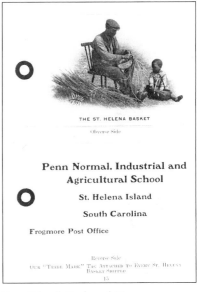

Penn School's Trademark Tag

George Brown

Price List from the 1924 *Annual Report*

hand, letting the dead, gray blades fall out. Then he would cure the rush outdoors in the sun until it turned a golden color, gathering and drying enough at one time so he wouldn't have to go out too often.

Penn's basketry students consumed a lot of materials and, as beginners, they naturally wasted some. If the students' work was not "up to standard," the School could not sell it. The work of some of the community basketmakers also fell below George Brown's high expectations. His son remembers him complaining, on occasion, that their knots were too conspicuous or their stitches irregular. To improve their technique, he encouraged Island basketmakers to work at the School's shop.

In 1916-17, making corn-shuck mats was added to the course of study. Sixteen of the forty-two boys in the Basketry Department learned this new skill. Again Penn's *Annual*

Report emphasized the economic incentive: "cash." Appealing to "all boys who hope to add to their earning capacity," the School offered to pay cash for work done at home.

Penn's basketry business declined during World War I. Production was handicapped by a scarcity of workers, "larger wages proving alluring to many of those who might have made baskets at home."[88] Some people left the Island as part of the northward movement of southern blacks that would become known as the Great Migration. While the enrollment of boys in the basketry shop did not fall until after the War, for the first time in fourteen years, the basket class of 1918-19 included girls—three students in the Normal (teacher training) program. Penn administrators might have been looking ahead to the need to prepare teachers to keep the craft alive. The School apparently felt the pressure of the wild inflation which followed the War. The basket instructor's salary increased three-fold, from $170.68 in 1917 to $580 in 1919, and by 1922 it had doubled again.

In the early 1920s, the shop's enrollment dropped by fifty percent, fluctuating between twenty-one and twenty-five boys. Still, the *Annual Report* claimed, the demand for baskets "has been steadily increasing." In 1924, 148 baskets and twenty-four corn-shuck mats were sold and seven chairs repaired, "artistic seats made from the corn shucks taking the place of broken cane." Five of Miner's photographs depicting baskets, basketmaking, and the gathering of rush were printed in this retrospective issue and, for the first time, so was a price list for St. Helena baskets.

With enrollment down to thirteen boys in 1928, the usually upbeat *Annual Report* expressed alarm lest Native Island Basketry "be allowed to become a lost art. This will happen," warned the *Report*, "unless Penn School can keep this shop open and interest the younger generation in it." On the eve of the Depression, basketry definitely was losing ground. People who in years past would have taken to the work were no longer willing to invest so many hours for such meager return. "I couldn't see no sense in it," Leroy Browne says, describing his own days as a student at Penn. "I spent six months in the basket shop and made half a basket."[89] At the prices baskets were bringing—$2 for a sewing basket, $10 to $12.50 for a clothes hamper—young people generally preferred to do something else. But it was not simply a question of economics. Southern farmers, black and white, were becoming aware of what life had to offer in other settings and other occupations. Penn's 1928 *Report* broached the difficulties of preserving a handcraft in modern times. "In this age of machines and speed," basketmaking was "slow and tedious work." Baskets themselves might be growing in "worth and popularity," but the kind of labor it took to make them was falling out of favor.

In order to economize, George Brown spent half his time on work other than basketry, "so that the spring demand is far in excess of supply." If the demand was not filled, people would stop asking for baskets. "This shop will have to go on full time if we are to preserve this craft," the *Report* concluded. True to their word, School personnel recruited more basketry students, increasing enrollment to thirty-one boys in 1929-30. A total of 108 sales in eleven different states was reported; sixty-nine of the baskets sold had been made in the community. Yet within two years, the School had to retrench again. At Miss Cooley's recommendation, Penn's trustees turned over the basketry, cobbling, and harnessmaking shops to the community, hoping that the two instructors would be able to supplement their half-time pay by doing community and farm work. But "under depression conditions," these craftsmen "found it difficult to find either work or cash, thus causing them serious personal problems."[90]

As hard times dragged on, the demand for St. Helena baskets diminished. Reflecting the general deflation that set in with the Great Depression, the price list of 1939 showed almost no increase over 1924 prices, and some styles—lunch baskets, hampers, and door mats—were actually selling for less. During World War II the basket shop was "kept busy caning chairs, doing corn shuck work, and always keeping a supply of baskets which are used in the school and shipped to fill orders." Howard Kester, who took over as Principal in 1944, claimed to have "secured several new outlets" for the products of the Basketry Department. But in his first year at Penn, only eight eighth-grade girls and no boys received instruction in the craft—a complete departure from tradition. George Brown was spending part of his time attending to the heating problems of the School. He continued to teach basketry until 1950, when Penn officially turned over its formal educational functions to the public schools. By this date, however, Native Island Basketry had ceased to be important to Penn. Basketry had been the steadiest and longest-running industrial course at the School. But

when "the twentieth century arrived on St. Helena sometime in the thirties," Penn's curriculum "had become an anachronism."[91]

Though the Penn School's protracted effort to preserve coiled basketry came to an end, Penn graduates had carried the craft to other places. From early in the century they had taught basketmaking at country schools and demonstrated it at field days on the Islands. On Daufuskie, Frances Jones remembers, she learned to make pine needle baskets from Sam Hazel, a St. Helena teacher.[92] Independent of Penn, other educators sought to keep alive basketsewing techniques. Sometime between 1926 and 1928, folklorist Robert Winslow Gordon photographed a basketry class near Darien, Georgia, supervised by one of his informants, Mary C. Mann. A deaconess in the Episcopal Church, Mary Mann ran a school that prepared young black women for domestic service. In Gordon's photograph, seven girls and a somewhat younger boy are working outdoors on small, oblong, coiled grass baskets.[93]

As late as the 1940s, coiled basketry was taught at Lincoln Public School in McClellanville, a coastal village about thirty-five miles north of Mt. Pleasant.[94] In places like McClellanville, the traditional craft had waned with commercial rice cultivation a generation before. Pine needles took the place of sweetgrass or rush because they were readily available and easier, perhaps, for students to handle. Their use represents a complex cross-cultural borrowing. Pine needle basketry was

George Brown's Chair

Basketmaking Class of Mary Mann. Photograph by Robert Winslow Gordon

Allen Green

practiced by various southeastern Indian peoples, who may have learned the technique from African American slaves;[95] by 1900 sewing pine needles with raffia had become a Victorian pastime, promoted by a spate of "how-to" books, "intended to instruct a predominantly middle-class female audience in how to spend their spare time fruitfully."[96]

The Last of the Old-Time Basketmakers

On St. Helena, Hilton Head, Daufuskie, and Sapelo Islands, the people who still make baskets or can remember a time when they did can be counted on one hand. "When I came along," says Allen Green, who was born in 1907, "boys and girls could make these baskets. Plenty could make it, but all die out. I'm the only one living so far."[97] About five years ago, to meet the demand for his work, Green taught his wife, Annie Mae, how to make baskets. Although sweetgrass grows profusely behind the beach on the ocean side of the Island, and rush is everywhere, the Greens use another marsh grass (possibly *Spartina patens*) in their baskets. They bind the rows with strips from the stems of the saw palmetto. Widely known as the last Georgians practicing coiled basketry, the Greens sell their baskets at a crafts fair on St. Simons Island each summer. Mr. Green sometimes demonstrates his technique to college students who come to his home on Sapelo. A large, red-lettered sign marks the end of his drive: "The Basket Weaver/Allen Green/Sapelo Island, Ga."

Caesar Johnson, of Hilton Head, learned to make baskets as a "tiny boy," around 1880. Seventy years later, his modest fame drew "many of the crafts-minded to his cabin." He also sold his wares through shops on Hilton Head, concentrating on four styles that proved most popular. Johnson lamented the passing of the art, explaining to a reporter in 1960 that "today's Negroes make more money at jobs," and don't want to practice a skill "that marks them as 'backwoods' or 'country.'"[98]

As recently as twenty years ago, at least two Hilton Head women—Beaulah Kellerson and Jannie Cohen—were selling their baskets on road stands along Highway 278. Mrs. Kellerson, now living in a nursing home on the Island, showed her baskets on the family's vegetable stand from the mid-'50s into the '60s. Her nephew, Abe Grant, recalls that when he returned from Miami in 1961, she was offering her big baskets for five dollars apiece. He advised her to double her prices, and he doubled the size of her display space.[99] Mrs. Kellerson made a variety of forms, including small trays, fanners, sifting baskets, magazine baskets, and covered clothes hampers. To make a space for the "metta," she used half of a scissors or a pocket knife. When a basket was finished she would soak it in water to tighten the rows. Many years before, she and her husband, William, had carried baskets to Savannah to sell along with fish and vegetables. Her son, Saul Grant, learned to sew baskets from her and her mother, Peggy Grant, but he no longer practices the craft. When he was growing up, men and women both made baskets on Hilton Head. They would cut "rushel" and dry it in the sun until it was "tender," Saul Grant says. Then it would "fold as easy as cloth."[100]

Jannie Cohen, who lives on the highway near the Grants, was taught basketmaking by her father, Ed Green. In the 1950s she, like Mrs. Kellerson, sold her baskets on the road—round ones, "egg-shell" or oblong ones, fanners, and trash baskets. She would nail a basket to a roadside sign which announced, "Baskets for sale." Asked who bought them, Mrs. Cohen replied, "Rich people, I reckon."[101] She remembers selling her fanners, each the size of a dishpan with three rows built up for sides, for three dollars. An enormous trash basket made by her and her brother, David Green, was photographed by a man from Augusta

Baskets by Beaulah Kellerson

who had commissioned it. It was one of the last baskets she made, about thirty years ago, until the autumn of 1985 when she was persuaded to make a basket for McKissick Museum. Since then she has gone back into more or less full-time production, using rush and strips of palmetto stem to produce sturdy, thick-coiled forms identical in construction to the oldest known examples of African American sea grass baskets.

The craft, as Caesar Johnson noted, is not being picked up by young people on the Sea Islands. Deterred, perhaps, by the low prices baskets were bringing even after the causeway brought droves of tourists to Hilton Head, and pushed by resort development and skyrocketing taxes to sell their land and move away, young Islanders have little incentive to work at traditional pursuits. Not only craft traditions but whole communities of people are threatened with extinction. "Developers come in and roll over whoever is there," says Emory Campbell, the current director of Penn Center. "We have given up on trying to protect the shrimp and crab because we, the black native population of these islands, have become the new endangered species."[102]

Mt. Pleasant "Show Baskets"

Why has coiled basketry persisted in Mt. Pleasant? The answer has to do with the strategic location of the community and the sewers' responsiveness to a new and growing market. Early in this century, people in Mt. Pleasant began making "show baskets" for sale to tourists and Charleston retailers. These differed from traditional agricultural or household "work baskets" in several ways: in the use of palm leaf instead of palmetto butt; in the proliferation of styles and decorative motifs; and in the basketmakers' concerted appeal to buyers. Adapting traditional forms and inventing new ones, sewers developed a large repertory of functional shapes—bread trays, table mats, flower and fruit baskets, shopping bags, hat box baskets, pocketbooks, church collection baskets, missionary bags, clothes hampers, sewing, crochet, and knitting baskets, spittoon baskets, wall pockets, picnic baskets, thermos bottles or wine coolers, ring trays, cord baskets, cake baskets, can baskets, wastepaper baskets, and platters in the shape of small fanners.

The sewers' first wholesale marketing venture was inaugurated in 1916 by a prominent Charleston merchant and civic leader named Clarence W. Legerton, whom basketmakers remember today as "Mr. Lester" or "Mr. Leviston." Through Sam Coakley, acting as an agent for basketmakers in his community, Legerton commissioned quantities of baskets and sold them both wholesale through his Sea Grass Basket Company and retail in his bookstore on King Street.

Legerton would come every other Saturday afternoon to Coakley's house in the Mt. Pleasant settlement of Hamlin Beach, where the sewers would have gathered with their baskets. Mary Jackson remembers being told that he would examine each basket "thoroughly all over" and "bang" on it "with his knuckles." He could tell by the sound if "it was a well-made basket."[103] "My mother used to make the basket and box them up and bag them up and take them over there," recalls Louise White, "and he'll go through and he'll get what he wants and he'll box them up and ship them away."[104] At that time, "a whole sheet" of baskets "didn't bring $12." Baskets were essentially dime-store items. Legerton's list price for small sewing baskets, for example, was $4.25 a dozen. Basketmakers knew he was selling their products by mail order, very rarely would he buy baskets with cross-handles, preferring instead compact shapes that could be packed easily for shipping.[105] But the sewers probably were not aware of the scale of Legerton's merchandising efforts.

In 1916-17, when he and his partners started the Sea Grass Basket Company, Legerton's basket purchases totalled $3,514.89, or over twelve percent of all the merchandise bought that year. Sales of baskets brought in $3,784.40, with $1,658.85 worth of baskets remaining in stock.[106] The next year he began keeping accounts of basket transactions on a separate page of his ledger. It appears that the Company's profits improved significantly. Legerton spent $3,770.73 on new stock, and sold baskets which had cost $2,950.88 for $4,390.81, realizing a gross profit of $1,439.93, or forty-nine percent over costs.

In 1920, Legerton changed the name of his basket business to Seagrassco. He continued to buy and sell thousands of dollars worth of baskets. This was most likely the year the Company stepped up its advertising campaign. Expenditures for stationery soared from $2.15 in 1919-20 to $184.33 in 1920-21, reflecting perhaps the cost of printing a mail

Jannie Cohen and David Green, ca. 1955

Clarence W. Legerton, ca. 1948

33

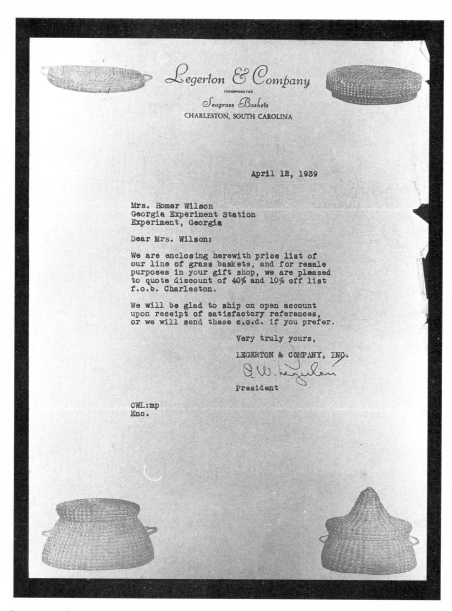

Legerton and Company Stationery

Sea Grass Basket Company Advertisement

order brochure and a special letterhead, which was illustrated with photographs of a different style of basket in each corner of the sheet.

Seagrassco's sales dropped by two-thirds in 1922-23, but its profit margin nearly doubled. In other words, the Company was selling many fewer baskets but charging more for each one. After deducting expenses, including commissions, advertising, and shipping, Seagrassco made a net profit of $893.73 in 1924-25—$600.01 in cash and $293.72 in baskets on hand—a year when Legerton & Company showed an operating loss of $1,837.33. Accounts indicate a markup of more than ninety-two percent; baskets purchased for $1,347.38 sold for $2,592.27. If the average list price of a basket was fifty cents, Seagrassco would have sold a total of about 5,000 baskets in 1924-25. Although the volume of sales tapered off, the basket business continued to be profitable at least through 1928, the last year for which accounts are available.

Consider what it must have meant to the small Hamlin settlement in the month of August, 1918, to receive $1,238.89 in payment for baskets. (This was the highest figure for any single month listed in Legerton's accounts. More typical monthly expenditures ranged from a few dollars to several hundred dollars.) In a farm community where cash was scarce and people produced most of what they consumed, $1,200 would have gone a long way, even divided as it must have been among many families.

As boys, Dr. Clarence W. Legerton, Jr., and his brothers once accompanied their father on a buying tour to New York. Dr. Legerton remembers the trip on a Clyde Line cruise ship, and a basket display in a New York department store, complete with a black woman demonstrating the sewing technique. His father, he says, was interested in local history and in promoting his adopted city of Charleston, but the bottom line of his basket business was profit.[107]

Early advertising copy for the Sea Grass Basket Company marked perhaps the first attempt to trace the origin and development of lowcountry basketry. An article in *The Picture and Art Trade and Gift Shop Journal* expressed admiration for the "talents" which basketmakers had "inherited from their forefathers."[108] Its dominant themes, however, were the backwardness of the blacks and the beneficial influence of the whites. Modern readers can recognize the mix of history and myth. For example, the fanner basket, according to this account, was invented by Negro slaves as a

Seagrassco Catalog

labor-saving device, to avoid work. Intended as a back-handed compliment, the notion is laughable, and the stereotype of the "proverbially lazy . . . genuine southern darky" contradicts everything we know about the backbreaking work required to cultivate rice. The article then adds insult to injury, attributing new basket styles to "interested parties" who "of recent years . . . have taught the negroes how to weave other and more complicated shapes."

Handsomely illustrated with photographs of a "double basket," a round tray with a cross-handle, and a covered sewing basket with wrapped sidehandles, the article describes the "pleasing and artistic" contrast "between the white strips of palmetto and the sage green grass." It stresses the limitations of production—the restricted range and season of sweetgrass and "the small number of negroes making strictly first grade baskets"—and claims that for several years "the output has been absorbed by local gift shops for sale to tourists and visitors." These baskets were offered "for the first time in quantities" in 1916,

and "owing to the shortage of foreign made baskets"—presumably because of World War I—Mt. Pleasant baskets were finding "a ready market."

Seagrassco's wholesale brochure is illustrated by the same baskets pictured in the trade magazine article, plus a covered cake basket and a bread tray with wrapped side handles.[109] The brochure gives prices for these and other styles of baskets in diameters ranging from five to nine inches: "Oval Baskets with Covers" (sewing baskets), "Oval Flat Baskets with Covers" (cake baskets), "Plate Shaped Trays" (fanners), round and oval "Table Mats," "Cord Baskets," "Pointed Cover Baskets" (steeple-top sewing baskets), a twelve-inch "Wall Pocket," a "Hand Bag with handles" (shopping bag), and a "Round Covered Basket with long handles" (hat box basket).

Most of these baskets were traditional forms, dating from the nineteenth century or possibly earlier. From David Doar's description, we know that double baskets were made before the Civil War; the sewing baskets on which they were based also date from the

Mary Jane Manigault, ca. 1971

plantation period. Circular hot plates originated in the 1890s or before.[110] Bread trays, flower baskets, and wall pockets were most likely innovations of the Victorian era.

One new element was introduced by Mr. Legerton sometime in the late 1930s—the use of colored thread as a binding material. On his trips to Mt. Pleasant he would distribute "some little plastic on a round spool and had people sewing colorful baskets—yellow, green, red, every color." Many sewers thought the baskets were "pretty," but they found sewing with the thread "a very hard job" because it was "too hard to get through the straw." Louise White remembers that for a while people struggled with the new material—"they had to do the best they can."[111] But they quit using it once Legerton stopped supplying it. Basketmakers today rarely use synthetic binders. They might experiment with the multi-colored wires from a telephone cable, or the yellow plastic strips used to tie plastic bags, or they might incorporate "found" objects, such as pop-tops from soda cans, between their rows. But these departures from traditional natural fibers are invariably short-lived.

Legerton continued to buy baskets directly from Mt. Pleasant sewers through the 1940s. His second son, Clifford, recalls that his father "tried his level best to get them to organize to mass produce."[112] No doubt, Clarence Legerton's steady patronage was a tremendous impetus to the basketmakers in and around Hamlin Beach, and may account for the settlement's heavy concentration of sewers.

"Manigault Corner," at one end of Hamlin Beach, consists of a dozen households with about sixty people.[113] Basketmaking is a habitual activity in most homes there, and as the girls mature many of them keep up the work. Mary Jane Manigault, an elder of the community and a daughter of Sam Coakley, Legerton's agent, is widely acclaimed as a master basketmaker. In 1984 she won a National Heritage Fellowship, a prestigious award given by the National Endowment for the Arts to draw attention to a lifetime of excellence in "a local tradition that has reached a really high level of artistry."[114]

Within fifteen years after Legerton began trading in Mt. Pleasant baskets, sewers developed a strategy for selling directly to tourists. The paving of Highway 17 and the construction of the Cooper River Bridge made the coastal route which passes through Mt. Pleasant a major north-south artery. Around 1930, basketsewers began displaying their wares on the road. Mrs. Betsy Johnson is reputed to have had the first "basket house" on the highway in front of her home. She and her daughter, Edna Rouse, would hang a few baskets from wooden "arms" nailed to a shed, to advertise that they had baskets for sale. To increase their stock, they would buy baskets from other sewers in the community. By the 1940s, Mrs. Johnson was commissioning work from numbers of people to fill "big orders," and sending "great boxes" of baskets away.[115]

"I set up a stand back when there weren't hardly any stands on the highway," recalled the late Irene Foreman in 1978. "Me and Hessie Huger set up a stand in 'Four-mile'"— neighborhoods in Mt. Pleasant are named for their distance from Charleston. "We figure we could make a whole lot more money than just sewing for Mr. Leviston. He'd pay twenty cents for a twelve-inch piece. If you sell them yourself you can get double that, all of fifty and seventy-five cents for a basket."[116]

The first basket stands were nothing more than a chair or overturned box placed on the edge of the road. Stands quickly evolved into a novel architectural form consisting of posts or saplings set upright in the ground, with thin strips of wood nailed horizontally between them. Nails served as pegs for hanging baskets. Sheds built behind the stands and outfitted with stoves, beds, and chairs provided some comforts for the basket sellers.

"I'd just get up in the morning and fix breakfast for my own self, and fix my lunch just like I was on a job, and go out to the

Basket Stand, Highway 17, Mt. Pleasant, 1986

stand," Miss Irene related. "Hessie Huger's husband would pick me up and come get us in the evening. We had a little house and all, with a bed in it and a stove. Why, we go out there and have a good time." Many sewers preferred the autonomy and amenities of selling from their own stands to the more exposed and hurried atmosphere of Charleston. "I didn't never sell no basket in the city. People go in one or two days, wanting to sell all, too. End of the day, they try to sell by lowering the price. I make better by sitting out to the stand and just take my time."

In the late 1940s, Mary Scott and a few friends devised a portable "three-leg stand," shaped like an "A" with one post in the center at the back. They set it up in "Four-Mile" to take advantage of being "closer to the tourists coming from Charleston." This invention gave them some of the maneuverability of a street vendor. "We could always pick it up and move it any time we get ready."[117]

Over the years, basketmakers have had many local patrons, but the chief clientele at basket stands always has been tourists. In 1949, the *News and Courier's* Jack Leland described "gleaming . . . automobiles, driven by persons from the large and modern centers of this country's industrial areas," who stop to look "at an importation of the artistry of African workers."[118] A photograph of "Betsy's Basket Shop" appeared above the article, showing Mrs. Johnson beside a display of some eighteen hat box baskets, as well as wall pockets, trash baskets, fruit and flower baskets, shopping bags, and table mats.

In the 1980s, tourist traffic flows past the basket stands twelve months a year. Today's stands look a lot like the old-time stands and sheds. Bare of baskets, they appear flimsy and make-shift, but in use they hold lively exhibitions of original art. Basketmakers may sit beside their stands, conversing with their neighbors, or sew in the privacy of their vans or station wagons, some of which are equipped with kerosene heaters, small televisions, and picnic coolers.

Despite these modern conveniences, selling on the highway entails risks and discomforts. High noise levels can make talking, even thinking, difficult. The danger of automobile accidents is real, with so many busy feeder roads emptying onto the highway and ever increasing commercial and residential traffic.[119] Air pollution irritates the people who stay at their stands all day and injures the baskets as well. Exposure to sun, rain, and dirt makes many baskets "go bad" before they can be sold.

Basket Stands on Highway 17, ca. 1977

Besides these possible misfortunes, sewers who don't own houses on the highway face the insecurity of not knowing whether they will be allowed to keep their stands where they are, or be forced to move them to make way for new condominiums or supermarkets.

On a given day, anywhere from a quarter to half of the stands may be in operation. Basket stands often are shared by several people, usually family members and friends, who display their baskets together or take turns selling at the stand. Basketmakers may buy baskets outright from other sewers who need ready cash or who don't have access to stands, and sell these baskets alongside their own. Some sewers bring their work out to the highway only occasionally. Others "hang out" their baskets on regular days of the week, or only in fine weather. Traffic—and sales—slack off in winter, and many basketmakers take the opportunity to work at home, using up their last supplies of cured grass and building up inventories for spring. A few invet-erate craftswomen can be found at their stands or street corners six days a week, winter and summer.

Despite the early success of the basket stands, sewers—especially those who didn't live on the highway—continued to sell whole-sale to local middlemen and retail shops. During the 1930s and '40s, Solomon Mazyck, a son of the beloved Maggie Mazyck, who was renowned as a basketmaker and a flower-grower,[120] carried Mt. Pleasant baskets on his horse-drawn wagon and peddled them door to door on Sullivans Island and the Isle of Palms. Judge Dennis Auld would buy quan-

Viola Jefferson, 1938

"The Hammock Shop," etching by James Fowler Cooper

game hunts in Africa, who asserted that African American baskets closely resembled in design and workmanship "those made by certain tribes today." Looking at the baskets, he claimed to be able to identify "from which of these ancestral tribes some of the Carolina descendants had sprung." The advertising copy acknowledged many "innovations" in the craft, some "very artistic, such as ingenious pine needle trim," others "startlingly grotesque." Waxing poetic, the brochure exclaimed that all were "beautifully executed and whiffing of the freshness of the sea."

The Hammock Shop's range of sweetgrass styles was similar to Seagrassco's earlier selection, suggesting that basket forms were rather stable through the 1930s. At $1.50, a "Cocktail Tray" containing seven coasters fastened to the bottom was the top of the Mt. Pleasant line. The price list includes three forms in bulrush and oak—waste baskets, fanners, and deep fanners—selling for $1, $1.25, and $2, respectively. Today, almost fifty years later, the Lachicotte family continues to carry sweetgrass baskets in their greatly expanded store, though traditional rush basketry in Georgetown County has indeed been "relegated to the lost arts." In recent years, Bea Coaxum, an accomplished Mt. Pleasant sewer, has been making the long drive to Pawleys in peak tourist seasons, to demonstrate and sell her work at the shop.

The basket brochures of the 1920s and '30s are valuable not only as attempts to give a history of the craft, but as artifacts themselves. They were produced by white people whose aim was to sell baskets, of course. But their motivation was not wholly commercial. In general, the publicists lamented the passing of the old-time plantation, along with the types of people the plantation had produced. They felt grief for the lost prosperity of rice culture and nostalgia for what they recalled as a tradition of paternalism. Though their racial ideas betray a profound misunderstanding of human biology, they nevertheless found something of value in the African past. Every article and brochure written about lowcountry baskets from 1900 forward identifies Africa as the home of these remarkable baskets.

In 1938, the Charleston Chamber of Commerce published a pamphlet entitled "An Art as Old as Africa."[124] "Hand-made Basketry, the Art of South Carolina Negroes," had become a selling point of "America's Most Historic City." Following two pages of text, the brochure listed twelve styles of baskets, with photo-

tities of baskets for his friend "Doc" Lachicotte to sell at his Hammock Shop on Pawleys Island, a beach resort sixty miles up the coast from Mt. Pleasant.[121] Established in 1938, this store specialized in local craftwork, including sea grass basketry, handmade Carolina pottery, rope hammocks, hooked and woven rugs, and hearth brooms. The Shop's first brochure, illustrated with photographs of merchandise and an etching by James Fowler Cooper, advertised a unique array of lowcountry baskets: old-time work baskets made of "bull rush bound with oak" side by side with Mt. Pleasant styles in sweetgrass and pine.[122]

The Hammock Shop's bulrush baskets were made by Welcome Beese, who had been born into slavery on Oatland Plantation, in All Saints Parish, Georgetown District, in the heartland of the antebellum rice kingdom. Beese was 104 years old when he was interviewed by Genevieve Chandler for the Work Projects Administration, in the late 1930s.[123] The Hammock Shop's brochure pictures him sitting next to an old mortar and pestle, against which are propped seven rush baskets. "The rice fanner, reminiscent of the good old days 'befo' de wa', will be relegated to the lost arts," predicts the brochure. "'Uncle Beese' sits. . . patiently weaving and, no doubt, meditates upon 'dese changeful times.'"

The Hammock Shop brochure emphasized the African origins of the sea grass basket, citing "an old white hunter," veteran of big

graphs, which could be ordered from the "Distributing Office" on Meeting Street. It also offered to take special orders—"either our designs or your specifications"—inviting patrons to suggest new ideas. "Hand Work Superior to Any Other Woven Work in America," the pamphlet proclaims. Like the broad "Gullah" dialect of the lowcountry Negro, the art of basketry is acknowledged to be an African survival. "Basketmaking had been handed down through the generations," passed on from the very old to the very young. "An old ex-slave woman, barely able to hobble with a stick," might be seen "teaching a great-grandchild . . . just learning to walk." The incentive to pursue the craft was chiefly economic: when children reached the age of four or five, they would be able "to make the simpler articles," and take their places "in the family, in earning the necessities of life."

The text makes a curious error, consistently referring to rush baskets, while the photographs clearly show sweetgrass forms decorated with pine straw. While pointing out the transition from "useful but not artistic" old-time baskets to the "more artistic designs and patterns" of contemporary work, the writer evidently had not caught on that basket materials had changed, too. While the Distributing Office dealt exclusively in sweetgrass forms, some rush baskets were being made for sale near Charleston in these years. "Down on Edisto Island live a few old Negroes who make baskets in their spare time. Here, strange to say, the weavers are mostly men," reported the WPA around 1940. They did not "go in for fancy design, either in color or shape," but were "content to make sturdy containers which may last a family over two generations." These Edisto sewers specialized in large clothes hampers, two-and-a-half to three feet high, which were sold for several dollars on order, and required a long time to make.[125]

Among the basket styles illustrated by the Distributing Office, six had cross-handles. A tall, cylindrical, footed "flower basket" is described as "conservative in design"—that is, an old form. A round, straight-sided "favor or fruit basket" resembles a bread tray with a cross-handle, rather than the flared form of the modern fruit basket. A covered "work basket" has straighter sides and a narrower base than a similar "crochet basket;" both forms have flat covers and high cross-handles. A tall "thermos bottle" or "jar basket" with gently in-sloping sides is advertised as "handy for the tourist or tripper." Probably a recent creation,

Boone Hall Plantation, ca. 1935. Photograph by Albert Sidney Johnson

the style was a variation on the older "can basket." A "shopping bag" is a deep, oblong basket with handles coming off either side of the top row. A "knitting basket" appears to be the form more commonly known as a hat box basket—round and straight-sided, with a hinged lid and long side handles extending from the cover and base. Five of the baskets are similar to ones wholesaled by Seagrassco: the "fruit basket" described above; the semi-spherical, covered "sewing basket" with wrapped side handles; the "dining table mats" in three sizes, one oblong and two round; and the eccentric "wall pocket—made in many patterns." The wall pocket pictured in the pamphlet is conical, with a wide border sewn to the back of the cone and two detached rows at the top for hanging. Also offered is a "serving basket" resembling the Hammock Shop's cocktail tray, except this one is fitted with openwork "rings," one row wide, rather than with cup-shaped coasters, to hold a decanter and six glasses. Technically complex and functionally specific, both sorts of "ring trays" are standard fare on highway stands today.

Like the Sea Grass Basket Company's advertising copy, the Distributing Office's pamphlet attributed the wide variety of basket patterns to white influence. Indeed, the two explanations of how these designs originated are so similar, one might guess that the 1938 text was based on the earlier account. Each describes recent innovations—"more complicated shapes," "more artistic designs and patterns"—as the result of coaxing by "the white folks of the lowcountry," under whose persuasion the old "utilitarian" articles became "decorative" too.

Baskets by Edna Rouse. Boone Hall Plantation, 1970

Cocktail Tray by Sue Middleton

While racially conceited and condescending in tone, this explanation contains an element of truth. Sewers and retailers alike were motivated to come up with styles which would appeal to their public. The thermos bottle basket and ring tray, for example, obviously were designed with the tourist and housewife in mind. Some styles no doubt were suggested by basket buyers or copied from objects basketmakers were shown; these practices are still common.[126] Recalling her trips to Charleston as a young girl to deliver her mother's baskets to a shopkeeper on King Street, Mary Jane Bennett explained that the lady would "draw the style she wanted on paper," and Mary Jane would bring it back to her mother, who would "look at it and . . . make it."[127]

Yet most forms were traditional. Ideal as souvenirs and gift items, sweetgrass baskets were products of an indigenous craft with a long history which, for some people, recalled the prosperous era of the rice plantation in the relatively impoverished present. Sewers rarely used these baskets themselves, preferring to sell everything they could. "In those times," says Mrs. Bennett, discussing the years of the Great Depression, you "couldn't afford to make the basket and keep 'em for yourself."

The claim that new styles were "taught" to sewers underestimates the basketmakers' capacity to create as well as to adapt, to improvise as well as to imitate. Even imitation is not a simple process. To produce a coiled basket in the shape of a container one has seen takes technical expertise which does not come easily. "You always gotta figure out your styles in your mind," Louise White explains.[128]

"Use" is Mrs. White's yardstick. She judges a basket by how well its form suits its function and whether it is strong enough to serve its purpose. Some contemporary sewers claim divine inspiration for their designs. When Greg Day and Kate Young stopped to ask about an openwork mat they saw on a stand, the basketmaker told them, "God gave me the idea to make it in a dream."[129] More commonly, innovations result from conscious aesthetic decisions. Mary Jane Manigault attached a ring of wrapped handles to an old-style cord basket for the first time in 1965.

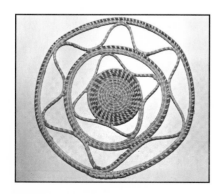

Star Wall Hanging (Cat. 29)

She considered this "ring of handles" to be "very beautiful" and later incorporated it into other basket forms.[130]

Day believes that a spiritual impulse underlies the "high degree of innovation and improvisation" of African American art. "Successful performance," he observes, is regarded by artists as "the result of the intuitive choice of alternatives presented to them by 'God' through their 'good mind.'" Poor choices, on the other hand, are "presented through their 'bad mind' which they believe to be 'ruled by the Devil.'"[131]

More than a set of religious ideas, these terms express a view of life and art. Young interprets "following your mind" to mean acting in accord with your "center, intuitions, life force, or spirit." To do this you must have your life in order, so that chaos and anxiety do not interfere with hearing your "good mind." The dictum of following your mind in daily life is so strong among the basketmakers of Mt. Pleasant, that no one feels bound very much by prior decisions or plans. "The present input of feelings, social situations, or just a strong sense of needing something else overrides other things," Young claims. "All women say as an explanation is 'my mind tell me to do—or not to do—this or that'. . . For black women living in an uncertain world with little power and influence, this philosophy has literally been a guiding light to safety, success, and artistry."[132]

Today, while few sewers describe the creative process in philosophic terms, the value placed on the development of "own style" baskets remains high. "An African craft that began with functional intentions," says John Vlach, "has become an art medium with primarily aesthetic motivation."[133] Freed from the utilitarian imperatives of the plantation era, and from the commercial restraints of early commission work which called for mass production of a limited number of styles, contemporary sewers are at liberty to follow their "good minds." Freedom and innovation go hand in hand. "You can make your basket the way you want and you can make 'em the price you want," says Evelyina Foreman, who as a youngster sewed for Legerton, as her mother had before her.[134]

Yet this does not mean that basketmakers have turned away from older forms. "I never look at pictures or study other basketry to come up with an idea," explains Mary Jackson. Rather, traditional styles are her main inspiration. "I could just go right from the same source that I already have. It's been there all along." What has not been there all along is the incentive to experiment. "I just think about a basket," Mrs. Jackson says. "I think about a shape and then I go and try to do it."[135]

The State of the Art

An activity that under slavery gave men a measure of independence, under freedom has provided economic opportunities and avenues of expression for women. The negative side of its persistence is that it reflects a reality of dismal alternatives. Until very recently, the only jobs available to black women in the lowcountry were poorly paid and menial, such as working in the fields or cleaning homes, hotels, hospitals, and restaurants. The women call these jobs "hard work," "working out," and "working for nothing."[136] Older basketmakers learned to sew when they were girls as an extension of farm life, in a tradition of independent producers and entrepreneurs. Some continue to make baskets because they must; besides being the best way they know to supplement their income, basketmaking has become so much a part of their lives they couldn't give it up. Maggie Polite Manigault, for example, explained to a granddaughter that she makes baskets "because she has been doing it for so long that she would feel lost if she didn't sew at least once a day."[137] Many younger women have returned to basketmaking after searching in vain for jobs that "pay something." Some have taken up the craft part-time while they are at home caring for small children or aging parents. Still others, drawn by the desirable qualities of the work, have chosen basketmaking over "outside" jobs. Basketmakers enjoy an autonomy which is rare in today's working world; they can set their own hours for weaving and selling, exercise their own judgment and intelligence, and work with family members in a collective enterprise.

Most sewers regard basketmaking first as a source of income, and their moods rise and fall with daily or seasonal fluctuations in sales. Some basketmakers—though generally not the youngest ones—find the work therapeutic. "Even though basketweaving is time consuming," says Mae Bell Coakley, "I enjoy it because it's relaxing, kind of therapy."[138] "Making things with your hands keeps your head together," Mary Jane Manigault reflects. "When you sew baskets, you just concentrate on that one thing. You have to have long patience. You can't be a nervous somebody and make baskets. You have to sit in one place and really

Maggie Manigault

get into what you are doing. You can't have your mind running on all kind of different things. You have to have a settled mind."[139]

Not the least of the satisfactions of making baskets is the chance to be paid and appreciated for doing your work well. While sewers unanimously complain that people don't want to pay what a basket is worth, basketmakers as a group have begun to enjoy a new status. "I think the biggest change," Jannie Gourdine told a Charleston journalist in 1980, "is that people look at us as artists now instead of just basket weavers."[140]

Coiled basketry has spread near and far as Mt. Pleasant women have married men from other areas or moved away pursuing jobs. Some sewers who have settled nearby, in communities such as Awendaw, McClellanville, Charleston, Johns Island, and Goose Creek, have enlisted the help of their husbands and in-laws in gathering materials, making baskets, and marketing. Other basketmakers moved to more distant South Carolina towns, such as Rock Hill, Sumter, and Frogmore, and as far away as New York City, Baltimore, Cartersville, Georgia, and Jacksonville, Florida. These emigrant sewers maintain close ties with home. Most acquire their materials and sell their baskets through relatives in Mt. Pleasant, and some spend summers there too.

Annabell Ellis and Florence Frazier

Basketmaking has expanded from settlement to settlement within Mt. Pleasant, as Mt. Pleasant itself has grown. In 1949, thirty-one stands were counted along a two-mile stretch of Highway 17, in the vicinity of Christ Church.[141] Today twice that many occupy sites on both sides of the road all the way from "Four-Mile" to "Ten-Mile." The number of highway shops peaked in the mid-'60s, when over seventy were reported. At this point sellers seem to have gotten ahead of their market. Sewers complained of too many stands, lower prices than five years before, and intense competition for the tourist trade.[142]

Few people could depend on basketmaking for a living. Most used it to supplement income earned doing housework or farm labor. "Some sell baskets in the winter and then work on a farm picking tomatoes and cucumbers in the summer," a basketmaker told a reporter for *The State* in 1966.[143] "Some days, don't make nothing," declared Victoria Milton, a sewer for over thirty years. "Some weeks, don't make nothing or make no more than four or five dollars." Apparently, basketmakers were earning about the same in the 1960s as they did in 1952, when the *Charleston Evening Post* estimated an average daily income at two dollars.[144] Medium-sized baskets were selling for two to three dollars, larger wastepaper baskets and picnic hampers for six or seven. Prices were slow to rise. In 1971, ten dollars was a top price for carry-alls,

serving trays, and handbags. "Just enough profit to keep body and soul together," sighed one long-time sewer. "The tourists won't pay any more than that because most of them figure that's all it's worth."[145]

Depressed prices were just one of the chronic problems afflicting the trade. By the 1970s, the number of basket stands had dropped to about fifty, with some 300 women engaged in the craft. Fewer stands did not mean a contracting market; instead, basketsewers were leaving the highway to try promising new outlets—craft shows, shops, galleries, commission work and, especially, the Charleston market. Nevertheless, observers felt that lowcountry basketry was in grave danger. "Rattlesnakes, a shortage of grass, and a lack of apprentices," reporter Tom Hamrick predicted, "will some day soon bring down the curtain on the centuries-old business of hand-woven basket making in Charleston County."[146]

Snakes always have been seen as a danger by the people who gather basket materials. To go into the "swamps" to pull sweetgrass, Mary Jane Bennett explained, "I used to put turpentine on my shoe. Snakes run from turpentine, and I just had to hope they didn't run toward me instead of away."[147] New and more serious threats to the craft were the scarcity of sweetgrass and the disinterest of the younger generation. As Mt. Pleasant developed into a sprawling suburb, local sources of sweetgrass were paved over or rendered off limits. Tropical storms and hurricanes which have struck the Carolina coast over the past few decades also have taken a toll on sweetgrass. Gatherers began travelling to Johns Island and Kiawah, but soon sweetgrass habitats in these places, too, were decimated by housing and resort development.

"I was fortunate enough to go on Seabrook Island before they started building up," Mary Scott relates, "and they had the beautifulest grass over there. Nobody knew about it till the people start surveying to get the golf course straight. . .and then our people saw the grass and we had a chance to get over there before the building start. The prettiest kind of grass you want to see was over there . . . and all these years those grass was there and nobody knew about them."[148]

At this critical juncture, in the early 1970s, Mt. Pleasant basketmakers again demonstrated their resourcefulness and versatility. Running short of sweetgrass, they rediscovered rush, and began using it to increase the strength and enhance the beauty of their baskets.

Although this "new" material has made up in part for the dwindling supply of sweetgrass, it has not replaced it as the basket's primary foundation material. Today, most sweetgrass comes from coastal Georgia and northern Florida, gathered for the basketmakers by men in their families or small-time entrepreneurs. The costs of these trips are borne by the sewers, who pay as much as twenty dollars for a bunch of grass you can just put your hands around. Even if they are able to recoup this expense when they sell their baskets, sewers have to plan for a major outlay of capital at the end of each summer, when they must stockpile enough grass to last until the gathering season begins in the spring.

The difficulty of interesting young people in the work—the second major threat to the craft's survival—has proved hard to overcome. The problem is two-fold: The sedentary nature of the work makes it unappealing to active youngsters, and its marginal economic rewards cannot compete with the legal minimum wage. "This is a boring way to spend all day," one basketsewer remarked, "and my children won't have nothing to do with basket-weaving." Predicting that the "business will die off" when the current generation dies, another basketmaker bluntly defined the trouble: "This is just too much monotony for the kids today. They don't want to sit all day and half the night and weave with their fingers and a little sawed-off spoon for a shuttle because they can make more money doing almost anything else."[149]

Children under the age of ten appear eager to learn to sew and feel privileged to participate in the work of their elders. As adolescents, however, they become preoccupied with social life, school work, television, and athletics, and they lose interest in the craft. "We don't want to sit down and do this kind of stuff," eighteen-year-old Melony Manigault confides. "We want to get up and go."[150] When pressed, some youngsters reveal a deep ambivalence about making baskets. On the one hand, they feel coerced and impatient when they are expected to sew. On the other hand, they know the importance of the craft to their parents and their people, and want to see it outlast their generation. Melony, for example, a serious girl and an heir to generations of sewers, expects to keep making baskets, "but not as steady as grandmama and mama." Sewing "one day out of the week," as she does, is "not good enough if you want to sell. You got to make 'em every day."

Mary Habersham at the Charleston Market

Kiawah, South Carolina

April Rivers

Sue Middleton

Edna Rouse

Melony plans to attend college and doesn't think she will live in the lowcountry after she graduates. By the age of thirty, women who have stayed in Mt. Pleasant usually have settled down and started raising families of their own. Many pick up basketmaking again as a means of earning a few extra dollars. Those who pursue the craft generally find compensations in the work other than money. "I just love to do it," says Sue Middleton, who quit her job about six years ago to sew full-time. Considering the time it takes to make a basket and the cost of materials, "you never get what you put in," she says. "If you're just doing it for the money, you'll never do it. You have to like it, too." [151]

Mrs. Middleton especially enjoys the independence the work affords, the opportunities for travel, and the pleasure of creating objects of beauty. Her baskets are exceptionally adventuresome. She turns out huge, heavily ornamented sewing baskets, four-sided market baskets, vases in the shapes of milk bottles and urns, as well as a full range of traditional styles. Equally at home with rush, sweetgrass, and pine, she often uses all three materials in one basket, though she makes an occasional form in pine alone. Mrs. Middleton prefers the solitude of her highway stand to the bustle of the market. But making baskets, for her, is also a social activity. One night a week, for the past several years, she has gotten together with half a dozen friends and relations at someone's house, to have a good time and sew.

The intrinsic rewards of the craft have been enhanced since the 1970s by an expanding public interest in African American folk art. Recognizing that sea grass basketry faced an uncertain future, folklorists and the media began descending on Mt. Pleasant, armed with notepads, cameras, and recording equipment. In 1971, South Carolina ETV produced a film entitled, "Gullah Baskets," documenting the African origins of the art and current threats to its survival. [152] The star of the show was Edna Rouse. Some basketmakers resented the term "Gullah," not wanting to be identified with a dialect generally regarded as backwards and incomprehensible. "I'm no Gullah," one woman protested. Another sewer, Eveline Nelson, stated that never in the forty years she had been sewing "have I ever heard them called Gullah baskets." But most basketmakers welcomed the publicity. "Anything which creates interest and causes tourists to stop is fine with me," Margaret Wilson explained. [153]

Meanwhile, lowcountry basketry and the community of sewers became the subjects of serious anthropological study. During the '70s, Mary Twining, Greg Day and Kate Young, John Vlach, Gerald Davis, Gloria Teleki, and Doris Derby conducted fieldwork among the basketmakers, studied the tradition, and wrote up their findings in scholarly articles and dissertations. [154] Twining established a basket collection at Indiana University, while Day and Young bought baskets for the Smithsonian Institution and the American Museum of Natural History. In field reports and photographs, they painstakingly portrayed the state of the art, just as it was experiencing a renaissance.

African American coiled basketry, along with Catawba Indian pottery, meanwhile enjoyed the attention of the South Carolina Arts Commission. [155] In the mid-'70s, the young and energetic staff of SCAC's Charleston Communication Center and Crafts Development Program recorded the basketmakers in photographs, slides, and audio- and videotapes. Hoping to expand the market for baskets, they distributed a mail order catalog featuring the work of five sewers, and published an accurate and perceptive pamphlet on the history of the craft, written by Greg Day. Basketmaker Mary Jane Bennett shared her knowledge and enthusiasm with SCAC filmmakers. As part of a travelling folk arts exhibit, she began attending craft shows and giving workshops in small towns around the state. "Things just been moving," she confirmed, "and I'm glad for it." [156]

Other Mt. Pleasant sewers were receiving high honors. In 1977, fifty baskets made by Mrs. Bennett, Bea Coaxum, and Marie Manigault were shown at the Smithsonian's Renwick Gallery in Washington, D.C., and Mrs. Coaxum attended a vice-presidential reception where four of her creations—a cup and saucer, a bell, and two stars—hung on Joan Mondale's Christmas tree. [157] John Vlach's path-breaking exhibition, "The Afro-American Tradition in Decorative Arts," marked the first major retrospective of the art. [158] In conjunction with Vlach's show, two Mt. Pleasant sewers, Celestine Turner and her daughter Ida Mae, were invited to demonstrate basketmaking at the National Museum of History and Technology as part of the Smithsonian's African American Arts Festival. [159]

Public acclaim has also come closer to home. In 1979, the College of Charleston showed a private collection of Mt. Pleasant baskets and in May, 1984, hosted an exhibit of Maggie Manigault's work, displayed against hand-woven textiles brought from Nigeria by her daughter, Lucille Akinjobi.[160] In November, 1984, the Gibbes Art Gallery opened a one-woman show of Mary Jackson's baskets.[161] Mrs. Jackson's mastery of traditional forms and her innovative designs had been honored before—her work had won prizes from the South Carolina Crafts Guild and had been exhibited at the Smithsonian's annual crafts fair and at the Vatican in Rome. But her show at the Gibbes was the first time that coiled sea grass baskets, which for centuries had appeared on the streets of Charleston, were exhibited in the halls of the city's most important gallery.

Coiled baskets appeal today to a broad and varied audience, from souvenir hunters to collectors of folk art, from people who want a bread basket to set on their dining table to museum curators who want to document the craft and preserve examples in dust-free, climate-controlled cabinets. Prices have risen dramatically since 1971, nearly doubling every five years. Small baskets now sell for ten to fifteen dollars, though most sewers keep on hand a number of two and five dollar items, such as bells, wreaths, Christmas stars, toy baskets, and the work of children. Middle-sized baskets range from twenty to eighty dollars, and very large baskets command prices in the hundreds and even thousands of dollars.

Considering the current market, sewers are more likely to spend the time making big baskets. Rush, with its thick blades and great rigidity, is structurally suited to large baskets, and encourages sewers to work on a grand scale. "I really love the large one now even more than I like the small one," says Marie Manigault, "because the large one show up prettier."[162] Grouped together on a display table at the edge of the highway, these big baskets catch the traveller's eye. They sell slower than small pieces, sewers report, but eventually they do sell

With their conical covers and big-bellied shapes, modern Mt. Pleasant baskets appear more African than earlier forms. Indeed, some sewers are influenced directly by exposure to African basketry, either through books or through examples of tribal crafts brought home by family members travelling abroad. In size and color, large contemporary baskets also bring to mind the traditional rush baskets that were used on rice plantations and family farms during the nineteenth century.

Several sweetgrass styles popular between the World Wars have become rarities—hat box baskets, double baskets, and hats, for example—but experienced sewers will make

Mazie Lee Coaxum

Mary Jane Bennett

Bea Coaxum

"The Cobra with Handle," by Mary Jackson

them on demand. Old-time cake baskets and sewing baskets have been transfigured into dozens of shapes and are decorated more highly than their predecessors. Yet most staples of the trade have remained virtually unchanged since the early 1900s. Like all traditions, basketmaking is inherently conservative. Basketmakers may take risks by modifying a style or by sewing an unusual form, but their standards of technique and performance do not vary. To the extent that these standards are respected, the most imaginative basket, one for which no practical use is envisioned, falls within the bounds of tradition.

Mt. Pleasant basketmakers tend to be guarded about their craft—protective of their livelihood and of a skill that sets them apart. "As long as nobody takes our baskets away from Charleston, from me and the black people here," Jannie Gourdine told a *New York Times* reporter in 1983, "then we'll never be obsolete. These baskets are part of us."[163] With the new public respect shown for their work, younger basketmakers have become less fearful than their elders about teaching the craft to people outside their community. Workshops in coiled basketry are offered regularly by museums, schools, adult education programs, and community centers throughout the lowcountry. In social profile, the people who attend these classes resemble the white middle-class women who filled the ranks of

the Arts and Crafts Movement at the turn of the century, and took up the art of Indian basketry as a pastime.

Basket classes may not produce many persevering sewers, but they instill in participants an appreciation of the physical and mental efforts that go into making a basket and a sensitivity to the enormous amount of work that is hidden in the finished product. From identifying the grasses in the field to gathering, hauling, cleaning, drying, and storing them; from hammering and filing a "bone" to starting the knot; from sewing a strong bottom to building up the sides and adding handles, covers, and decorative elements; from shaping a basket in one's imagination to realizing the shape with one's hands— the steps in making a basket require time, skill, and concentration. True, the actual sewing is repetitious, like laying a course of bricks. The sewer sits still for hours at a time, but her hands and her mind are always in motion.

Coiled basketry survived the loss of its old functions because basketmakers found new ones and developed the aesthetic side of their tradition. The hand production of baskets remained feasible because sewers did not expect more than marginal income from it, and because there were few competing opportunities. As economic prospects for black people improve, basketmaking will become less appealing as a way to earn an income. Yet, by enduring into the 1980s, sea grass basketry has become subject to forces which make its immediate future bright. Charleston's tourist traffic shows no sign of let-up, and the flow of potential buyers is expanded because of the convention trade. A small collectors' market underwrites the trend toward greater recognition and higher prices. How many people the demand for baskets-as-art can support is uncertain, but the impact of this new market is likely to be greater than one would guess from the limited number of sewers who cater to it. We can already see the tendency toward larger, more showy baskets; the emphasis on regular stitching and elaborate surface decoration; the rise of innovation and the eclipse of the basket's historic provincialism and primitivism—the results, albeit indirect, of pressures and tastes exerted by buyers looking for expressive forms.

As society becomes more technical and craft skills become the province of specialists, the value of handmade objects will increase. Mt. Pleasant basketmakers should see more income from their craft, and those who want to may be able to spend more time sewing.

Basket Workshop at the Gibbes Art Gallery, Charleston

Many sewers will never be adequately paid for their time and labor. The hidden costs in a basket are simply too great. But regardless of market conditions, some people will continue to sew. As tokens of loved ones and links between the generations, baskets are meaningful to them in ways buyers cannot fathom.

Louise White, a reflective and devoted basketsewer, explained that while she was keeping house for a certain family she would examine a set of sweetgrass placemats her mother had made many years before. If she found a place that needed repair she would "carry a palm from home in my pocketbook" and mend the break, "just to see how long Mama basket will be there." She plans to give each of her children an example of every type of basket she makes, hoping to provide them with models from which to sew. "I always want them to have something to remember in days to come," she muses. Perhaps they will be inspired to take up where she leaves off. "It may be hard for them to see it, but days will come when they will sew baskets. . . .This basket here is strictly just in the lowcountry, and if the generation don't take it up when we gone, it's going to die away. But they will sew baskets. They will, time will come, they will sew."[164]

Baskets are live and eloquent forms, firmly rooted in a lineage and a tradition. In a world of abrupt shifts and dislocations, the old shapes and techniques have always been elements of stability. One can sew a familiar form and transcend the insecurity of the moment. Making a basket takes self-discipline; it gives self-possession. Even if the basket serves someone else's purpose, the act of sewing connects the basketmaker to a proud inheritance that cannot be diminished.

Louise White

Notes

1.   Governor James Glen quoted in Peter H. Wood, *Black Majority: Negroes in Colonial South Carolina from 1670 through the Stono Rebellion* (New York, 1974), p. 58.

2.   Rice was introduced into North Carolina in the 1720s with the settlement of the Lower Cape Fear River by a group of wealthy South Carolina planters. James M. Clifton, "Golden Grains of White: Rice Planting on the Lower Cape Fear," *The North Carolina Historical Review*, 50:4(October, 1973), p. 365. By the mid-1700s the "golden grain" was also grown on a small scale in the Savannah River basin and on St. Simons Island, Georgia. A great expansion of the crop occurred in the 1830s and '40s, when many Carolina planters extended their activities down the coast of Georgia as far as northern Florida. Albert V. House, ed., *Planter Management and Capitalism in Ante-Bellum Georgia* (New York, 1954), pp. 20-21.

3.   House, p. 53. For a far-ranging discussion of the origins of rice culture in the southern tidewater, see J. Leitch Wright, Jr., *The Only Land They Knew* (New York, 1981), p. 263.

4.   Mary Jane Manigault, personal communication, January 16, 1985.

5.   Since 1896, when A. W. Chapman classified *M. filipes* as a variety of *M. capillaris*, most botanists have followed suit, with two notable exceptions. T. H. Kearney (1900) did a comparative study of the internal leaf anatomy of the two plants and concluded "that in *M. filipes* we have a perfectly valid species." H. L. Blomquist (1948) agreed that "it seems best to consider this grass a distinct species." In 1971 Joseph Pinson and Wade Batson found *M. filipes* to be "morphologically distinct from *M. capillaris* on the basis of size and floret structure." The two grasses were also distinguished by different flowering times and habitat requirements. "These differences in morphology, physiology, and ecology," Pinson and Batson declared, "strongly support the maintenance of *M. filipes* as a valid species." Joseph N. Pinson, Jr., and Wade T. Batson, "The Status of *Muhlenbergia Filipes* Curtis (Poaceae)" in *The Journal of the Elisha Mitchell Scientific Society*, 87:4(Winter, 1971), pp. 188-191. Robert E. Perdue, Jr., mistakenly identified sweetgrass as *Sporobolus gracilis* in 1968. See "'African' Baskets in South Carolina," *Economic Botany*, 22:3(1968), pp. 289-292. In the following years the error was repeated in several accounts of lowcountry basketry. James Bishop, in correspondence with Joseph Pinson, set the record straight in letters dated June 26, July 27, July 31, and August 2, 1979. See correspondence in collection of James M. Bishop. Sweetgrass is correctly identified as *M. filipes* in Wilbur H. Duncan and L. E. Foote, *Wildflowers of the Southeastern United States* (Athens, Ga., 1975), p. 234; and in Joseph N. Pinson, Jr., "A Floristic Analysis of Open Dunes in South Carolina" (Ph.D. diss., University of South Carolina, 1973), p. 12.

6.   Interview with Louise White, Awendaw, S.C., February 13, 1985.

7.   Ed Rossbach, *Baskets as Textile Art* (New York, 1973), pp. 106-120.

8.   Interviews with Saul Grant, Hilton Head, S.C., August 1, 1985; and Leroy E. Browne, Sr., Frogmore, S.C., November 21, 1985.

9.   For a contemporary description of splitting oak, see Eliot Wigginton, ed., *The Foxfire Book* (Garden City, N.Y., 1972), pp. 115-118.

10.   Jeannette Lasansky, *Willow, Oak, and Rye: Basket Traditions in Pennsylvania* (University Park, Pa., 1979), pp. 25, 29.

11.   In the coiled basketry of all cultures, awls were traditionally made of bone. In Germany, awls were made from antlers. Dan Freas, Old Salem, N.C., personal communication, May 31, 1985. In southern Appalachia, basketmakers used "a rear leg bone of an old horse," and made a second tool from "a straight section of cow horn. . . for shaping the coils of straw." Sue H. Stephenson, *Basketry of the Appalachian Mountains* (New York, 1977), p. 37. Native American used the leg bone of a deer.

12.   Interviews with Louise White; Marie Manigault, Mt. Pleasant, S.C., February 8, 1985; and Florence Mazyck, Mt. Pleasant, S.C., July 23, 1985.

13.   Interview with Leroy Browne.

14.   John Michael Vlach, *The Afro-American Tradition in Decorative Arts* (Cleveland, Oh., 1978), p. 7.

15.   Gregory K. Day and V. Kay Young (Kate Porter Young), "Preliminary Field Report," Smithsonian Institution, Washington, D.C., 1971, Item no. B.5.4.

16.   *Ibid.*, Item no. C.12.3.

17.   *Ibid.*, Item no. C.7.1.

18.   Interview with Barbara McCormick, McClellanville, S.C., March 8, 1985.

19.   Day and Young, Item no. C.36.1.

20.   Edith M. Dabbs, *Face of an Island: Leigh Richmond Miner's Photographs of St. Helena Island* (Columbia, S.C., 1970), n.p. George Brown used the same lashing technique to attach a twisted strip of chair caning material as a handle on a sewing basket.

21.   Day and Young, Item no. C.14.1.

22.   *Ibid.*, Item no. C.17.3.

23.   Gregory Day, "Afro-Carolinian Art, Towards the History of a Southern Expressive Tradition," *Contemporary Art/Southeast,* 1:5 (January/February, 1978), p. 19.

24.   Interview with Helen Gadsden and family, Awendaw, S.C., March 30, 1985.

25.   Interview with Marie Manigault.

26.   Interview with Mae Bell Coakley, Mt. Pleasant, S.C., February 12, 1985.

27.   Interview with Mary Jane Bennett, Mt. Pleasant, S.C., March 22, 1985.

28.   Interview with Joseph Foreman, Mt. Pleasant, S.C., October 23, 1985.

29.   "Forty-three percent of the Africans brought into South Carolina during the eighteenth century came from regions where rice was an important crop." Daniel C. Littlefield, *Rice and Slaves: Ethnicity and the*

Slave Trade in Colonial South Carolina (Baton Rouge, La., 1981), p. 113. Lowcountry planters "were willing to pay higher prices for slaves from the rice-growing region of West Africa—what they called the 'Rice Coast'—and particularly from Sierra Leone." Joseph Opala, quoted in "The 'Gullah' connection," *West Africa*, May 19, 1986, p. 1046. See also, "Sierra Leone has S.C. ties," *Charleston Post/Courier*, January 5, 1986.

30. Margaret Trowell and K.P. Wachsmann, *Tribal Crafts of Uganda* (London, 1953), p. 134.

31. Mary A. Twining, "Harvesting and Heritage: A Comparison of Afro-American and African Basketry," *Southern Folklore Quarterly*, 42 (1978), p. 167; Vlach, p. 16. The issue of the specific origins of Afro-American sea grass basketry demands a great deal more study. Africanist Stanley Alpern several provocative questions about the links between lowcountry baskets and rice-growing areas of Africa. Personal communication, November 24, 1986, and May 14, 1987.

32. A notice in the Charleston *Gazette and Advertiser* on February 15, 1791, for example, announced the public auction of "A Negro Man, who is a good jobbing carpenter and an excellent basket maker, sold for no fault, but that of having a sore leg." South Caroliniana Library, Columbia, S.C. [SCL]

33. William Gibbons's Account Book, 1765-1782, Georgia Historical Society, Savannah, Ga. [GHS]

34. Interview with Allen Green, Sapelo Island, Ga., August 2, 1985.

35. Some slaves "found both pleasure and profit in using their leisure to pursue a handicraft; they made brooms, mats, horse collars, baskets, boats, and canoes." Kenneth M. Stampp, *The Peculiar Institution: Slavery in the Ante-Bellum South* (New York, 1956), p. 367.

36. Theodore Rosengarten, *Tombee: Portrait of a Cotton Planter, with the Journal of Thomas B. Chaplin*, 1822-1890 (New York, 1986), p. 530.

37. *Ibid.*, p. 403.

38. James Potter's Journal for Argyle Plantation, September 18, 1828 and August 18-21, 1830, GHS.

39. Interview with Allen Green.

40. David Doar, *Rice and Rice Planting in the South Carolina Low Country* (Charleston, S.C., 1936), p. 33.

41. Journal of Thomas Walter Peyre, 1834-1851(?), South Carolina Historical Society, Charleston, S.C. [SCHS]

42. James Potter's Journal, August 15-27, 1831.

43. Elizabeth W. Allston Pringle, *Chronicles of Chicora Wood* (Boston, 1940), pp. 53-54.

44. Day, "Afro-Carolinian Art," p. 21. In an earlier will the abbreviation "fann." probably meant "fanners." Day, personal communication, June 3, 1985.

45. Elaine Herold, personal communication, May 10, 1985. Ms. Herold conducted this excavation for the Charleston Museum in the early 1970s.

46. Leland Ferguson, personal communication, April 26, 1985. Underwater sites are anaerobic, that is, without oxygen, and therefore do not support organisms which normally cause plant fibers to decay.

47. Dr. E. Elliott quoted in Doar, *Rice and Rice Planting*, p. 18.

48. Alexander S. Salley, Jr., ed., *Narratives of Early Carolina, 1650-1708* (New York, 1967), p. 69, n. 2.

49. David Doar, *A Sketch of the Agricultural Society of St. James, Santee, South Carolina and an Address on the Traditions and Reminiscences of the Parish Delivered before Society on 4th of July 1907* (Charleston, S.C., 1908), p. 11.

50. Quoted in Wood, *Black Majority*, p. 79.

51. James M. Clifton, ed., *Life and Labor on Argyle Island: Letters and Documents of a Savannah River Rice Plantation, 1833-1867* (Savannah, Ga., 1978), p. xxv.

52. Doar, *A Sketch of the Agricultural Society*, p. 11. Rice cultivation required great outlays of capital, and only the wealthiest planters could afford the new technology. Successful rice plantations might represent a total investment of between $50,000 and $500,000. Clifton, *Life and Labor*, p. xiii. The cost of steam-powered threshing mills—$8,000 by the 1850s—meant that most of the rice produced in Georgia and North Carolina, and much grown in South Carolina, continued to be threshed by hand flail. Not everyone who could afford to mechanize did so. Nathaniel Heyward, "the greatest of all rice planters," for example, "long continued to have his crops threshed by hand, saying that if it were done by machines his darkies would have no winter work; but when eventually he instituted mechanical threshers, no one could discern an increase of leisure." Ulrich Bonnell Phillips, *American Negro Slavery* (Baton Rouge, La., 1966), p. 249.

53. Clifton, *Life and Labor*, p. xxiv.

High-Handled Covered Basket (Cat. 23)

49

54. House, p. 62. In Edmund Ruffin's *Report of the Commencement and Progress of the Agricultural Survey of South Carolina* (Columbia, 1843), p. 118, winnowing was not listed among the "usual tasks" assigned to rice hands—an indication that this process had been mechanized on most plantations. See also, "Rice Lands of South Carolina," *Harper's New Monthly Magazine*, November 1859, p. 730.

55. Charles Joyner, *Down by the Riverside: A South Carolina Slave Community* (Urbana, Ill., 1984), p. 52. Charles Manigault, who purchased Gowrie Plantation on the Savannah River in 1833, usually gave his "people" there broken rice worth $2.50 a bushel in reward for good service. Phillips, p. 255.

56. Elizabeth Hyde Botume quoted in Dena J. Epstein, *Sinful Tunes and Spirituals: Black Folk Music to the Civil War* (Urbana, Ill., 1977), p. 163.

57. Alice R.H. Smith, selected watercolors reproduced and annotated in a special edition, George Rogers, ed., SCL. Originally published in Herbert Ravenel Sass, *A Carolina Rice Plantation of the Fifties* (New York, 1936), n.p. D.E. Huger Smith, *A Charlestonian's Recollections, 1843-1913* (Charleston, S.C., 1950), p. 15.

58. Vlach, p. 16.

59. Doar, *Rice and Rice Planting*, pp. 33-34.

60. Day, "Afro-Carolinian Art," pp. 13, 19. Day also attributes the Charleston triple chest and the Charleston single house to African influences—a claim that is hotly disputed.

61. Vlach, p. 13.

62. Lasansky, p. 22. "In 1893 alone, Lichtenfels, Germany, exported to the United States baskets valued at $192,000, many of them being willow."

63. Day and Young, Item nos. B.3.2.(A) and B.13.1.

64. A bamboo fan covered with "crazy" patchwork and fitted with a pocket might be used to keep rooms tidy "by holding items such as magazines, dustcloths, letters, and hairbrushes that needed to be within reach, but that would add to the clutter if left out." Penny McMorris, *Crazy Quilts* (New York, 1984), p. 15. Wall pockets served the same functions as splintwork "half baskets," or "key baskets," which in the antebellum era were hung on the wall of plantation Big Houses to contain "keys, combs, mail, or other small items." Lasansky, pp. 40-41, Stephenson, p. 20. Southeastern Native Americans also made wall-hanging baskets, in conical and elbow shapes. It is difficult to say which of these traditions simply shared an affinity with the coiled grass wall pocket, and which may have influenced its development.

65. Interview with Marie Manigault.

66. *Anti-Slavery Reporter*, ser. 3, XII, September 1, 1864, pp. 202-203, reprinted in John Blassingame, *Slave Testimony: Two Centuries of Letters, Speeches, Interviews, and Autobiographies* (Baton Rouge, La., 1977), pp. 449-454.

67. Interview with Frances Jones, Hilton Head, S.C., November 23, 1985. See also, Fran Smith, "Daufuskie 'mayor' loves island's peacefulness," *The Island Packet*, February 4, 1982. "As Frances' great-grandmother told the story, the migration of black families. . . was accomplished. . .in a small fleet of rowboats, each handled by eight men."

68. Interview with Allen Green.

69. House, p. 78. In the second half of the nineteenth century, Burma was to become the world's leading exporter of rice. David Moltke-Hansen, personal communication, April 25, 1986.

70. Kay Young Day (Kate Porter Young), "My Family Is Me: Women's Kin Networks and Social Power in a Black Sea Island Community" (Ph.D. diss., Rutgers University, 1983), pp. 14-15.

71. Postcard entitled "Women Vegetable Venders, An Every Morning Scene on the Streets of Charleston, S.C.," SCHS. The lowcountry Afro-American language, known as Gullah, is considered by many linguists to be "the only surviving creolized form of English spoken in the United States." It was the speech of the Negro population of the Sea Islands and tidewater region, "roughly from Jacksonville, North Carolina, to the mouth of the St. Johns River in Florida." By 1860, perhaps 100,000-150,000 people spoke Gullah, and a hundred years later, possibly twice that number. Today, "Gullah is in rapid process of decreolization, and practically all its speakers are able to shift between dialect and an approximation of standard English. Gullah has obvious links, historical and structural, with West Indian creole English." John E. Reinecke, *A Bibliography of Pidgin and Creole Languages* (Honolulu, 1975), p. 468. For a recent analysis of Gullah, see Joyner, pp. 196-224.

72. *The Exposition,* Charleston, S.C., 1901, p. 470, SCL.

73. Savannah Unit, Georgia Writers' Project, Work Projects Administration, *Drums and Shadows: Survival Studies Among the Georgia Coastal Negroes* (Athens, Ga., 1940), p. 8.

"African" Cord Basket (Cat. 43)

74. Charlotte Smith, "The Last of the Old-Time Basket Makers," *Savannah News,* July 17, 1960.

75. Rufus Saxton, Federal military commander at Port Royal, quoted in Elizabeth Jacoway, *Yankee Missionaries in the South: The Penn School Experiment* (Baton Rouge, La., 1980), p. 26, n. 6.

76. Jacoway, p. 43.

77. *Ibid.*, p. 10.

78. McDavid Horton, "Negro Island Farmers Are Unique Community," reprint from *The State* (Columbia, S.C.), January 17-20, 1924, p. 14.

79. *Annual Report of the Penn Normal, Industrial, and Agricultural School,* 1910, p. 15, SCL.

80. Dabbs, n.p. This double-pen house consists of two rooms of unequal size with a front and back door opposite each other. The layout is English, the scale Afro-Caribbean. John Michael Vlach, personal communication, April 5, 1986.

81. Jacoway, pp. 124, 125. For a view of African retentions in Negro music on St. Helena Island in the Civil War era, see William Francis Allen, Charles Pickard Ware, and Lucy McKim Garrison, *Slave Songs of the United States* (New York, 1951), pp. i-xx.

82. *Annual Report,* 1924, p. 32.

83. Jacoway, p. 88.

84. Rossa Cooley quoted in Horton, p. 6.

85. *Annual Report,* 1916, p. 23; Horton, p. 14.

86. *Annual Report,* 1914, p. 14.

87. Interviews with Leroy Browne, November 9, 1984 and November 21, 1985.

88. *Annual Report,* 1919, pp. 17-18.

89. Interview with Leroy Browne, November 9, 1984.

90. Jacoway, p. 221.

91. *Ibid.*, p. 219.

92. Interviews with Frances Jones, August 1, 1985 and November 23, 1985.

93. *"Folk-Songs of America:" The Robert Winslow Gordon Collection, 1922-1932,* Neil V. Rosenberg and Debora G. Kodish, eds., The Archive of Folk Song, Library of Congress (Washington, D.C., 1978), p. 13.

94. Edna Wynn, personal communication, January 25, 1986.

95. The material culture of African and Native American tribal peoples had many elements in common—mortars and pestles, pottery, calabashes, dugout canoes, nets, basketry, as well as other objects. There was considerable contact between the two groups and a significant incidence of intermarriage, but it is difficult to assess the influence their craft tradi-tions had on each other. For a discussion of Native American basketry as "a supportive element" of the "African-derived" coiled tradition, see Vlach, p. 16.

96. Tim Bookout, "Review of the Literature," unpublished typescript, (Atlanta, n.d.), p. 28.

97. Interview with Allen Green.

98. Smith, "The Last of the Old-Time Basket Makers."

99. Interviews with Abe Grant, Hilton Head, S.C., August 1, 1985 and November 23, 1985.

100. Interviews with Saul Grant, August 1, 1985 and November 23, 1985.

101. Interview with Jannie Cohen, Hilton Head, S.C., August 1, 1985.

102. Quoted in "Cultural Activity in the Sea Islands," *Highlander Reports,* newsletter of the Highlander Folk Center, New Market, Tenn., November 1984.

103. Interview with Mary Jackson, Charleston, S.C., August 24, 1985.

104. Interview with Louise White.

105. Interview with Maggie Manigault, Mt. Pleasant, S.C., March 27, 1985.

106. "Business Record" of Legerton & Co., collection of John E. Huguley [JEH]. The following accounts of the Sea Grass Basket Company are found in these papers.

107. Interview with Dr. Clarence W. Legerton, Jr., Charleston, S.C., July 2, 1985.

108. "Sea Grass Baskets An Interesting Industry," *The Picture and Art Trade and Gift Shop Journal,* n.d. (1918), JEH.

109. "'Seagrassco' Hand Made Baskets," collection of Clifford L. Legerton.

110. Day and Young, Item no. C.52.2. A small, worn, coiled disc, made of rush and sewn with oak splits, used at Cat Island Plantation on the Santee River and donated to the Charleston Museum in 1919, also suggests that the hot plate was a nineteenth century form.

111. Interview with Louise White.

112. Clifford L. Legerton, personal communication, July 9, 1985.

113. Young, "My Family Is Me," p. 5.

114. Bess Lomax Hawes, director of the National Endowment for the Arts Folk Arts Program, quoted in Edward D. Murphy, "Lowcountry Artisans Chosen for National Award," *Charleston News and Courier,* September 7, 1984.

115. Interview with Blanche Watts, Mt. Pleasant, S.C., July 26, 1985.

116. Kate Porter Young, fieldnotes, 1978.

117. Interview with Mary Scott, Mt. Pleasant, S.C., June 19, 1985.

118. Jack Leland, "Basket Weaving African Art Survival?" *News and Courier,* March 27, 1949.

119. Interview with Mary Scott.

120. Beulah Glover, "Diversified Farming Makes Maggie Mazyck Independent," Walterboro *Press & Standard,* April 8, 1934; Irma L. Bennett, "Basket Making in the Low Country" (several drafts), April 4, 1940, WPA Federal Writers' Project, S.C., Charleston County School Stories, SCL; "Maggie Mazyck, Flower Vendor, Dies at 83," *News and Courier,* January 24, 1961.

121. Dennis Auld, Jr., personal communication, March 30, 1985; interview with A.H. Lachicotte, Jr., Pawleys Island, March 24, 1986.

122. "The Hammock Shop, Gifts & Novelties from the Carolina Low Country," n.d. (1939), SCL. For a reproduction of Cooper's print, "The Hammock Shop," see no. 78, in Boyd and Stephanie Saunders, *The Etchings of James Fowler Cooper* (Columbia, S.C., 1982).

123. Joyner, caption of photograph ff. p. 126.

124. "Hand-Made Basketry, the Art of South Carolina Negroes," n.d. (1938), pamphlet issued by the Distributing Office, Charleston, S.C., collection of Laura Sloan Crosby.

125. Bennett, "Basket Making in the Low Country."

126. "The Negroes generally make up their own designs," WPA researchers reported around 1940, "but once in a while customers suggest a particular shape or a different color scheme. The basket makers are apt pupils. The design is soon added to their store of patterns." "Basket Making in the Low Country" (Washington Revised Copy), WPA Federal Writers' Project, Charleston County, S.C., SCL.

127. Interview with Mary Jane Bennett.

128. Interview with Louise White.

129. Day and Young, Item no. C.2.1(A).

130. *Ibid.,* Item no. C.14.1.

131. Day, "Afro-Carolinian Art," p. 10.

132. Kate Young, personal communication, April 7, 1986.

133. Vlach, p. 19.

134. Interview with Evelyina Foreman, Mt. Pleasant, S.C., October 23, 1985.

135. Interview with Mary Jackson.

136. Young, "My Family Is Me," p. 21.

137. Veronica Washington, "Basket Weaving: From a Source of Income to a Hobby," unpublished paper, College of Charleston, 1985.

138. Interview with Mae Bell Coakley.

139. Kay Young, fieldnotes, 1977.

140. "Jannie Gourdine," *Post/Courier,* October 26, 1980.

141. Leland, "Basket Weaving African Art Survival?"

142. "Basket Weaving Continues to Thrive in Lowcountry," *News and Courier,* July 29, 1964.

143. Betty Sadler, "'People Stop and Talk; Some Buy—Some Don't,'" *The State,* March 11, 1966.

144. Walter Crews, "Negro Craftsmen Ply an Ancient Art by the Side of a Bustling Highway," *Charleston Evening Post,* June 27, 1952.

145. Tom Hamrick, "Old Craft Is Dying Out," *The State,* May 16, 1971.

146. *Ibid.*

147. Quoted in Lisa Hammersly, "South Carolina Basket Makers Battling Hard Times," *Charlotte Observer,* July 26, 1981.

148. Interview with Mary Scott.

149. Hamrick, "Old Craft is Dying Out."

150. Interview with Melony Manigault, Mt. Pleasant, S.C., June 12, 1985.

151. Interview with Sue Middleton, Mt. Pleasant, S.C., July 2, 1985.

152. Elizabeth McRae Scroggins, "Gullah Baskets," S.C. ETV Guide, April 1, 1971.

153. Hamrick, "Old Craft Is Dying Out."

154. Besides works previously cited, see: Gerald L. Davis, "Afro-American Coil Basketry in Charleston County, South Carolina," in *American Folklife*, Don Yoder, ed. (Austin, Tx., 1976), pp. 151-184; Mary A. Twining, "An Examination of African Retentions in the Folk Culture of the South Carolina and Georgia Sea Islands" (Ph.D. diss., Indiana University, 1977); Gloria Roth Teleki, *Baskets of Rural America* (New York, 1975), and *Collecting Traditional American Basketry* (New York, 1979); Doris Adelaide Derby, "Black Women Basket Makers: A Study of Domestic Economy in Charleston County, South Carolina" (Ph.D. diss., University of Illinois, 1980).

155. Margaret Locklair, "New Program Markets State Handcrafts," *Post/Courier,* May 1, 1977; "Handcraft Guild," *Evening Post,* May 6, 1977.

156. Quoted in Bill Robinson, "Facing South," n.d. (1977), Charleston County Library, Charleston, S.C.

157. "Lowcountry Arts Again Get National Recognition," *Evening Post,* December 8, 1977; "Local Baskets on Exhibit at Smithsonian," *News and Courier,* December 8, 1977; "Basketmaker's Ornaments Adorn Mondales' Tree," *The State,* December 18, 1977; "Basketmaker Is Guest at Mondales' Reception," *Evening Post,* December 23, 1977.

158. The exhibition toured nationally from 1978 through 1979. Besides basketry, it included examples of Afro-American musical instruments, woodcarving, quilting, pottery, boatbuilding, blacksmithing, architecture, and graveyard decoration.

159. Robert Small, "Basket Weavers D.C.-Bound," *News and Courier,* October 16, 1979; "Basket Weavers," *News and Courier,* November 7, 1979.

160. "A Selective Listing of Lowcountry Trends and Events," *Post/Courier*, August 5, 1979; "Lowcountry Basket Exhibit on Display," *Post/Courier*, May 27, 1984.

161. "Lowcountry Art," *Post/Courier,* November 18, 1984; Elsa F. McDowell, "Mary Foreman Jackson Weaves Works of Art," *Post/Courier*, December 9, 1984.

162. Interview with Marie Manigault.

163. Quoted in Skip Rozin, "The Handmade Baskets of Charleston," *New York Times,* February 13, 1983.

164. Interview with Louise White.

Fanner Basket, Mary Jane Manigault

Catalog of Exhibition

Fanners (Cat. 5, 4, 3, 2)

*All baskets, unless otherwise noted, are from South Carolina.
23-55 are Mt. Pleasant baskets.*

1. Colleton District Fanner Basket
unknown maker, ca. 1850
H.2 5/8" W.17 1/8"
Coiled straw (possibly rice) and
corn shuck sewn with splits (possibly oak).
Clare P. McWhirter, Walterboro, South Carolina

2. Santee River Fanner Basket
unknown maker, Wedge Plantation, ca. 1890
H.3 1/2" W.19 1/4"
Coiled rush sewn with oak splits.
Amy Lofton Moore, Charlotte, North Carolina

3. Upper St. John's Parish Fanner Basket
unknown maker, Numertia Plantation, n.d.
H.3 1/8" W.15"
Coiled straw sewn with oak splits.
Harriet Clarkson Gaillard, Camden, South Carolina

4. Cooper River Fanner Basket
unknown maker, Wapoolah Plantation, n.d.
H.3 1/2" W.21 1/4"
Coiled rush sewn with oak splits.
The Charleston Museum, Charleston, South Carolina

5. Fanner Basket
unknown maker, Georgia, nineteenth century
H.5 3/8" W.23"
Coiled straw (possibly rice) and corn shuck sewn
with oak splits.
Julia Floyd Smith, Savannah, Georgia

6. Waccamaw River Fanner Basket
attributed to Welcome Beese, ca. 1935
H.4 5/8" W.20 1/2"
Coiled rush sewn with oak splits.
*Alberta Lachicotte Quattlebaum, Pawley's Island,
South Carolina*

7. Fanner Basket
Caesar Johnson, Hilton Head Island, ca. 1950
H.3 1/4" W.16 1/8"
Coiled rush sewn with strips of palmetto butt.
Agnes L. Baldwin, Summerville, South Carolina

8. Fanner Basket
Blanche Watts, Mt. Pleasant, 1986
H.2 1/2" W.17 7/8"
Coiled rush sewn with palmetto leaf.
McKissick Museum, Columbia, South Carolina

9. Small Round Basket
unknown maker, Wedge Plantation, ca. 1890
H.3" W.7 1/8"
Coiled straw sewn with strips of palmetto butt.
Amy Lofton Moore, Charlotte, North Carolina

Fanners (Cat. 6,7)

Vegetable Basket (Cat. 10)

10. **Georgetown District Vegetable Basket**
     unknown maker, Kinloch Plantation, ca. 1900
     H.6 3/4" W.27 1/4"
     Coiled rush sewn with oak splits.
     McKissick Museum

Vegetable Basket (Cat. 11)

11. **Vegetable Basket**
     unknown maker, Georgia, ca. 1900
     H.4 1/2" W.21 1/4"
     Coiled marsh grass sewn with strips of palmetto butt.
     Tim Bookout, Atlanta, Georgia

12. **Memminger School Diploma Basket**
     unknown maker, n.d.
     H.6 5/8" W.17 1/2"
     Coiled rush sewn with strips of palmetto butt.
     South Carolina Historical Society, Charleston, South Carolina

Diploma Basket (Cat. 12)

13. **Sewing Basket With Strap Handle**
     George Brown, St. Helena Island, ca. 1930
     H.8" W.10 1/2"
     Coiled rush sewn with strips of palmetto butt and vine handle.
     Leroy E. Browne, Sr., Frogmore, South Carolina

14. **Oblong Basket**
     Caesar Johnson, Hilton Head Island, ca. 1950
     H.3 3/4" W.11 5/8"
     Coiled rush sewn with strips of palmetto butt.
     Agnes L. Baldwin

Sewing Basket (Cat. 15)

15. **Sewing Basket**
     Allen Green, Sapelo Island, Georgia, 1985
     H.5 3/4" W.10 3/4"
     Coiled marsh grass sewn with strips of palmetto butt.
     McKissick Museum

16. **Sewing Basket**
     Frances Jones, Hilton Head Island, 1985
     H.3 3/4" W.8"
     Coiled pine needles sewn with green and pink raffia.
     McKissick Museum

17. **Round Basket**
     Jannie Cohen, Hilton Head Island, 1985
     H.5 3/4" W.14"
     Coiled rush sewn with strips of palmetto butt.
     McKissick Museum

18. **Work Basket**
     unknown maker, n.d.
     H.2 3/4" W.5"
     Coiled sweetgrass and pine needles sewn with palmetto leaf.
     The Charleston Museum, Charleston, South Carolina

Round Basket (Cat. 17)

19. Cake Basket
unknown maker, n.d.
H.3 5/8" W.17 1/4"
Coiled sweetgrass and pine needles sewn with palmetto leaf.
The Charleston Museum, Charleston, South Carolina

20. Covered Sewing Basket
unknown maker, n.d.
H.3 1/4" W.6 3/4" L.6 3/4"
Coiled straw sewn with palmetto leaf. Fabric lined.
Tim Bookout

21. Sewing Basket
unknown maker, ca. 1930
H.5" W.7 7/8"
Coiled sweetgrass and pine needles sewn with palmetto leaf.
Louise Levi Marcus, Eutawville, South Carolina

22. Cross-Handled Basket
unknown maker, ca. 1930
H.10 1/2" W.9"
Coiled sweetgrass and pine needles sewn with palmetto leaf.
Harriet Clarkson Gaillard

23. High-Handled Covered Basket
Josephine Coakley, 1979
H.13 1/4" W.10"
Coiled sweetgrass and pine needles sewn with palmetto leaf.
McKissick Museum, Crosby Collection

24. Small Ring Tray
Cathy Johnson, 1979
H.1 1/2" W.9"
Coiled sweetgrass and pine needles sewn with palmetto leaf.
McKissick Museum, Crosby Collection

25. Wall Pocket
Cathy Johnson, 1979
H.8 3/4" W.9"
Coiled sweetgrass and pine needles sewn with palmetto leaf.
McKissick Museum, Crosby Collection

Pail Basket (Cat. 26)

26. Pail Basket With Double Hinged Handles
Irene Foreman, ca. 1979
H.9" W.7"
Coiled sweetgrass and pine needles sewn with palmetto leaf.
McKissick Museum, Crosby Collection

Sewing Basket (Cat. 21)

Hat and Missionary Bag (Cat. 27, 28)

27. **Broad-Brimmed Hat With Hat Band**
Irene Foreman, 1980
H.5" W.15"
Coiled sweetgrass and pine needles sewn with palmetto leaf.
McKissick Museum, Crosby Collection

28. **Missionary Bag**
Irene Foreman, 1980
H.16 1/4" W.12"
Coiled sweetgrass and pine needles sewn with palmetto leaf.
McKissick Museum, Crosby Collection

29. **Star Wall Hanging**
unknown maker, ca. 1980
W.17 1/2"
Coiled sweetgrass and rush sewn with palmetto leaf.
McKissick Museum

30. **Food Storage Basket**
Janie Mazyck, 1982
H.8" W.19"
Coiled sweetgrass and rush sewn with palmetto leaf.
McKissick Museum

Food Storage Basket (Cat. 30)

31. **Sewing Basket**
Florence Mazyck, 1982
H.6 1/2" W.12"
Coiled sweetgrass, rush and pine needles sewn with palmetto leaf.
McKissick Museum

32. **Needlework Basket**
Martha Johnson, 1982
H.12" W.10"
Coiled sweetgrass and pine needles sewn with palmetto leaf.
McKissick Museum

Needlework Basket (Cat. 32)

33. **Fruit Basket**
Elizabeth Mazyck, 1982
H.14" W.12"
Coiled sweetgrass, rush and pine needles sewn with palmetto leaf.
McKissick Museum

Wastebasket (Cat. 34)

34. **Waste Basket**
Henrietta Snype, 1984
H.7 1/2" W.12"
Coiled sweetgrass and pine needles sewn with palmetto leaf.
McKissick Museum

35. **Cake Basket**
Joseph Foreman, 1984
H.2 3/4" W.10"
Coiled sweetgrass and pine needles sewn with palmetto leaf.
McKissick Museum

36. **Sewing Basket**
Evelyina Foreman, 1985
H.5 1/4" W.12"
Coiled sweetgrass and pine needles sewn with palmetto leaf.
McKissick Museum

Sewing Basket (Cat. 40)

Sewing Basket (Cat. 36)

37. **Sewing Basket**
Mary Jackson, 1985
H.5 3/4" W.13"
Coiled rush, sweetgrass, and pine needles sewn with palmetto leaf.
McKissick Museum

38. **Hat Box Basket**
Yvonne Foreman, 1985
H.4 3/4" W.15 1/2"
Coiled sweetgrass and pine needles sewn with palmetto leaf.
McKissick Museum

39. **Bread Basket**
April Rivers, 1985
H.2 1/2" W.9"
Coiled sweetgrass and pine needles sewn with palmetto leaf.
McKissick Museum

40. **Sewing Basket**
Mary Scott, 1985
H.6 1/2" W.10 1/2"
Coiled sweetgrass and pine needles sewn with palmetto leaf.
McKissick Museum

41. **Candy Dish**
Tiffany Scott, 1985
H.1 1/2" W.6 1/2"
One-Handed Hot Pad
Michelle Scott,
1985
H.1/4" W.9"
Two-Handed Tray
Latoyana Scott, 1985
W.6 3/4"
Hot Pad With Single Handle
Meggan Scott, 1985
W.6 1/2"
Coiled sweetgrass and pine needles sewn with palmetto leaf.
McKissick Museum

42. **Flower Vase**
Sue Middleton, 1985
H.11 3/4" W.10"
Coiled sweetgrass, rush, and pine needles sewn with palmetto leaf.
McKissick Museum

Flower Vase (Cat. 42)

43. **"African"Cord Basket**
Helen Gadsden, 1985
H.14" W.10 1/2"
Coiled sweetgrass and pine needles sewn with palmetto leaf.
McKissick Museum

44. **Open Hamper**
Florence Mazyck, 1985
H.11" W.11 1/4"
Coiled sweetgrass, rush, and pine needles sewn
with palmetto leaf.
McKissick Museum

45. **Fruit/Flower Basket**
Blanche Watts, 1985
H.15" W.10"
Coiled sweetgrass sewn with palmetto leaf.
McKissick Museum

48. **Star Bread Basket**
Mae Bell Coakley, 1985
H.2 3/4" W.10 1/2"
Coiled sweetgrass and pine needles sewn with palmetto leaf.
McKissick Museum

Star Bread Basket (Cat. 48)

49. **Triple-Decker Yarn Basket**
Louise White, 1985
H.12" W.10"
Coiled sweetgrass and pine needles sewn with palmetto leaf.
McKissick Museum

50. **Double Basket**
Mary Jane Manigault, 1985
H.9 3/4" W.13 1/2"
Coiled sweetgrass and pine needles sewn with palmetto leaf.
McKissick Museum

51. **Shopping Bag**
Maggie Manigault, 1985
H.16 1/2" W.15 1/4"
Coiled sweetgrass, rush, and pine needles sewn
with palmetto leaf.
McKissick Museum

Fruit/Flower Basket (Cat. 45)

46. **Casserole Holder**
Mary Vanderhorst, 1985
H.3 3/4" W.11 1/2"
Coiled sweetgrass, rush, and pine needles sewn
with palmetto leaf.
McKissick Museum

47. **Flower Basket**
Sharod Carlton Rouse, 1985
H.9 1/2" W.6"
Coiled sweetgrass and pine needles sewn with palmetto leaf.
McKissick Museum

Shopping Bag (Cat. 51)

Market Basket (Cat.52)

54. "Four Corners" Fruit Basket
Estelle Rouse, 1986
H.12" W.11"
Coiled sweetgrass and pine needles sewn with palmetto leaf.
McKissick Museum

55. "Two Lips" Basket
Mary Jackson, 1986
H.18 1/2" W.15 1/8"
Coiled sweetgrass and rush sewn with palmetto leaf.
Charles and Louise Pettis, Hilton Head Island, South Carolina

52. Market Basket
Jessie Bennett, 1985
H.16 1/2" W.17"
Coiled sweetgrass, rush and pine needles sewn
with palmetto leaf.
McKissick Museum

53. "Egg-Shaped" Basket
Annabell Ellis, 1985
H.18 1/2" W.9"
Coiled sweetgrass and rush sewn with palmetto leaf.
McKissick Museum

"Two-Lips" Basket (Cat. 55)

Acknowledgements

A definition of folk art is difficult to produce. Just what objects can be considered art and what specific qualities make them "folk art" are subjective. As museum curators, collectors, or writers we make our pronouncements on this subject in relation to our observation of the dynamic equilibrium between the aesthetic and utilitarian dimensions of objects. Our evaluation of the practical and formal intentions that are integral to the process of creation leads each to a personal determination. Leaving aside our individual decisions on what is and what is not "folk" in its traditions or of artistic merit, we are brought again face-to-face with the objects. The baskets in this exhibition speak for themselves. They are both utilitarian and beautiful. Moreover, the various forms created by these basketsewers through their technical mastery of materials are reflections of the community in which the baskets were made and which imposes upon them a system of economic, social, and cultural practices.

An awareness of the complex interrelationship between the object and its environment has been a strong component of this project since its inception. Beginning with the first acquisition in 1978 of six baskets by then curator Eugenia Seibels from Greg Day, the Museum's staff has been aware of the cultural and aesthetic significance of these objects. The enthusiasm for both building a major collection and documenting the tradition has come from George D. Terry, now the Museum's director and formerly the curator of the historical collections.

Ann Salter and Kevin Bowers authored the Youth Grant from which this project grew. Funding came, however, from the National Endowment for the Arts, Folk Arts Program, where Bob Teske provided valuable assistance in helping us formulate our goals. Bess Lomax Hawes, director of the Folk Arts Program, became an enthusiastic supporter and wise counselor. This project would never have come to fruition, however, without the intelligence and devotion of Dale Rosengarten. Attentive to both the historical roots of this tradition and to the accomplishments of the basketsewers, she has transformed a modest one-year project to document the work of basketmakers into a major resource on this folk art form. She has discovered valuable original source materials, especially early photographs and documents, and through hours of interviews documented the contemporary artists.

The Museum's basket collection now numbers over 200 pieces. As the focus of the exhibition, which this catalog accompanies, these objects will be used by scholars, writers, and museum curators for years to explore the rich tradition of South Carolina's folkways. Mark Smith, as registrar, provided the necessary work for preparing the collection.

The success of the exhibition at its initial showing at McKissick Museum during the fall of 1986 prompted the staff to organize a traveling schedule which would allow other interested museums to share in this project. Catherine Wilson Horne, the curator of the Museum's collection, was responsible for the exhibition at McKissick and the reorganization of the works into a new pre-sentation. The Museums Program at the National Endowment for the Humanities provided support for an extensive interpretive program to further the understanding of this important craft. Within that organization Suzi Jones provided much help to us in articulating our ideas about the significance of this project. Barbara Tartaglia coordinated the program with the borrowing institutions. Cece Byers Johnson authored the education materials. Many other people, including Dale Rosengarten, Mary Jackson, Paul Figueroa, Nancy Nusz and Theresa Singleton gave freely of their time as lecturers or consultants.

In the same manner that this exhibition and catalog are only a part of the whole basket project, so the project is only a part of the Museum's folk arts programming. The office of the State Folk Arts Coordinator at McKissick is ably directed by Gary Stanton. He has consistently provided us with expertise, and, more important, kept us aware of the wider social significance of these art objects.

The financial support which converted our enthusiasm and intellectual curiosity into a meaningful reality came from the National Endowment for the Arts, Folk Arts Program; the South Carolina Arts Commission; the National Endowment for the Humanities; and the University of South Carolina. The support of all these organizations, both monetary and technical, was extremely valuable.

Lynn Robertson Myers
Project Director
McKissick Museum

Sewing Basket (cat. 16)

The gracious cooperation of many people has made my work a fruitful and joyous adventure. My thanks go first and foremost to the basketmakers who welcomed my interest in their art and gave freely of their time and expertise. Not only those listed as participants in the project, but also many of their relatives and friends, contributed materially to my research. I am especially grateful to Mary Jackson, Sue Middleton, Henrietta Snype, Mary Vanderhorst, Blanche Watts, Estelle Grant, and Marie Manigault for their friendship, encouragement, and advice.

I have followed in the footsteps of a number of intrepid fieldworkers. James M. Bishop, Timmy Joe Bookout, Laura Sloan Crosby, Gregory Day, John Michael Vlach, Mary A. Twining, and Kate Porter Young have shared the results of their research and offered their guidance. For helping me understand the historical and cultural dimensions of lowcountry baskets, I am indebted to James M. Clifton, Leland Ferguson, Glenn Hinson, Charles Joyner, Roger Manley, and Peter H. Wood.

Much of the chronicle of lowcountry basketry lies in the private papers and memories of families who have witnessed that history. For their patience and trust in answering my questions and allowing access to their collections, I want to thank Dennis and Barbara Auld, Jr., Agnes L. Baldwin, Priscilla B. Baldwin, Anne L. Bridges, Leroy E. Browne, Sr., Harriet C. Gaillard, Nancy G. Guthridge, Abe Grant, Lillian Grant, Saul Grant, Tony Grant, Louise Johnson Guy, John E. Huguley, Catherine Tupper Jessen, Allison L. Koelling, A.H. Lachicotte, Jr., Dr. Clarence W. Legerton, Jr., Clifford L. Legerton, Jack Leland, Louise L. Marcus, Dr. and Mrs. McKensie P. Moore, Robert Morgan, Genevieve C. Peterkin, Charles and Louise Pettis, Samuel D. Prentiss, Michael and Virginia Prevost, Alberta Lachicotte Quattlebaum, Julia Floyd Smith, and Clare P. McWhirter.

In my search for old photographs, documents, and baskets, I have had the able assistance of Emory S. Campbell at the Penn Center, Judith Wragg Chase at the Old Slave Mart, David Moltke-Hansen and Susan Walker at the South Carolina Historical Society, Chris Loeblein, Martha Zierden, and Sharon Bennett at the Charleston Museum, Martha R. Severens at the Gibbes Art Gallery, James A. Fitch at the Rice Museum, Frank McNutt at the South Carolina Arts Commission, Gurdon Tarbox and Robin Salmon at Brookgreen Gardens, Allen Stokes at the South Caroliniana Library, and Michael Trinkley at Chicora Foundation, Incorporated.

At McKissick Museum, I have received consistently excellent support from George D. Terry, Lynn Robertson Myers, Catherine Wilson Horne, and Mark Smith. Ann Ferebee Brown, Darcy Wingfield, and Tom Cowan have worked long and productive hours on the project. My thanks also go to Gary Stanton for keeping us all on course.

A special note of gratitude to my friends: to Billy Baldwin for his critical eye, to John McWilliams and Jan Arnow for their camera work, to David Bruck, Beverly Leichtman, and Laura Lee Wilson for their hospitality, and to Katherine Wells Scholtens for her good cheer and companionship. Everlasting appreciation goes to Theodore Rosengarten, my editor-in-chief and constant guide.

Dale Rosengarten
Guest Curator
McClellanville, S.C.

Dale Rosengarten Measuring a Basket

Bibliography

I. Museum Collections

American Museum of Natural History, New York, N.Y.

Charleston Museum, Charleston, S.C.

Daughters of the Confederacy Museum, Charleston, S.C.

McKissick Museum, Columbia, S.C.

Old Slave Mart Museum, Charleston, S.C.

Rice Museum, Georgetown, S.C.

Smithsonian Institution, Washington, D.C.

South Carolina State Museum, Columbia, S.C.

William Mathers Anthropology Museum, Bloomington, Ind.

II. Manuscripts, Pamphlets, and Government Documents

"Basket Making in the Low Country" (Washington Revised Copy). WPA Federal Writers' Project, Charleston County, S.C. South Caroliniana Library, Columbia, S.C. [SCL]

"Basketweaving: A Unique Art." Souvenir booklet. Mt. Pleasant: Mt. Pleasant Exchange Club, July 22, 1944. McKissick Museum, Columbia, S.C. [MM]

Bennett, Irma L. "Basket Making in the Low Country" (several drafts). WPA Federal Writers' Project, S.C., Charleston County School Stories (April 4, 1940). SCL.

Bookout, Timmy Joe. "Review of the Literature." Unpublished typescript. Atlanta: n.d. (1985).

"Business Record" of Legerton & Co. Collection of John E. Huguley. [JEH]

Crafts Development Program. *Lowcountry Sweetgrass Baskets.* Columbia: South Carolina Arts Commission, 1978.

"Cultural Activity in the Sea Islands." *Highlander Reports,* Newsletter of the Highlander Folk Center. New Market, Tennessee, November 1984.

Day, Gregory K., and V. Kay Young [Kate Porter Young]. "Preliminary Field Report." Smithsonian Institution, Washington, D.C., 1971.

Day, Gregory K. *South Carolina Lowcountry Coil Baskets.* Charleston: The Communication Center, South Carolina Arts Commission, 1977.

The Exposition. Charleston, S.C., 1901. SCL.

William Gibbons' Account Book, 1765-1782. Georgia Historical Society, Savannah, Ga. [GHS]

"The Hammock Shop, Gifts & Novelties from the Carolina Low Country," n.d. (1939). SCL.

"Hand-Made Basketry, the Art of South Carolina Negroes." Pamphlet. Charleston: Distributing Office, n.d. (1938). Collection of Laura Sloan Crosby. [LSC]

Herndon, Estella S. "Basket Making." WPA Federal Writers' Project, Orangeburg County, S.C., 1936. SCL.

Kefalos, Roberta. Mary Jackson: Lowcountry Baskets. Pamphlet. Charleston: Gibbes Art Gallery, 1984.

Journal of Thomas Walter Peyre, 1834-1851(?). South Carolina Historical Society, Charleston, S.C. [SCHS]

James Potter's Journal for Argyle Plantation. GHS.

Robinson, Bill. "Facing South," n.d. (1977). Charleston County Library, Charleston, S.C.

Rosengarten, Dale. "Fieldnotes and Interviews, Lowcountry Basket Project." Unpublished manuscripts, 1985. MM.

"Sea Grass Baskets An Interesting Industry." *The Picture and Art Trade and Gift Shop Journal,* n.d. (1918). JEH.

"Seagrassco Hand Made Baskets." Catalog and price list. Collection of Clifford L. Legerton.

Smith, Alice R.H. Selected Watercolors from *A Carolina Rice Plantation of the 1850s.* Reproduced, annotated, and edited by George Rogers. SCL.

Tobias, Rowena W. "Basket Weaving." WPA Federal Writers' Project, Charleston County, S.C., n.d. (1936). SCL.

Twining, Mary A. "Interviews and Works in Progress." Unpublished manuscripts. William Mathers Anthropology Museum, Bloomington, Ind., 197___.

Washington, Veronica. "Basket Weaving: From a Source of Income to a Hobby." Unpublished paper, College of Charleston, 1985. MM.

III. Newspaper and Magazine Articles

"Ancient Art on Display." *Evening Post.* Charleston, S.C. 21 July 1974.

"Basket Artisanry." *Evening Post.* 18 October 1976.

"Basket Case." *News and Courier.* Charleston, S.C. 3 September 1975.

"Basket Handcraft." *News and Courier.* 24 April 1971.

"Basketmaker Is Guest at Mondales' Reception." *Evening Post.* 23 December 1977.

"Basketmaker's Ornaments Adorn Mondales' Tree." *The State.* Columbia, S.C. 18 December 1977.

"Basketweaver." *Evening Post.* 23 April 1980.

"Basket Weavers of Charleston." *Southern Living* (October, 1970): 22, 26.

"Basket Weaving Continues to Thrive in Lowcountry." *News and Courier.* 29 July 1964.

Charleston Gazette and Advertiser, 15 February 1791. SCL.

"Craft, Art Show in Charlotte This Weekend." *The State.* 6 December 1984.

Crews, Walter. "Negro Craftsmen Ply an Ancient Art by the Side of a Bustling Highway." *Evening Post.* 27 June 1952.

DeWolf, Karol K. "Low Country Baskets." *Country Home* 8:5(October 1986): 67-73.

"ETV Documentary to Air Art of Basket Weavers." *News and Courier.* 25 April 1971.

"Flower Women Number More Than Sixty." *News and Courier.* 12 January 1947.

Frazier, Herbert L. "Basketweaving Traced to Ancient African Craft." *News and Courier.* 4 September 1972.

"Free Access to Market Stalls Brings Back Scenes of Old Time Activity to the City's Venerable Food Exchange." *News and Courier.* 2 September 1935.

Glass, Mary A. "Licensing Stalled at City Market." *News and Courier.* 3 October 1976.

Glover, Beaulah. "Diversified Farming Makes Maggie Mazyck Independent." Walterboro *Press & Standard,* 8 April 1934.

[Grovsner], Verta Mae. "What Does South Carolina Lowcountry Mean To Me? Home!" *Washington Star.* Washington, D.C. April 1971.

"The 'Gullah' Connection," *West Africa.* 19 May 1986.

Hammersly, Lisa. "South Carolina Basket Makers Battling Hard Times." *Charlotte Observer.*

Hamrick, Tom. "Old Craft Is Dying Out," *The State.* 16 May 1971.

"Handicrafts, Films To Be Added to Park." *News and Courier.* 17 January 1972.

Horton, McDavid. "Negro Island Farmers Are Unique Community." *The State.* 17-20 January 1924.

Huff, Bobbin. "Weaver Hopes to Perpetuate Craft." *Evening Post.* 9 October 1974.

"In-and-Out Basket Goes to California." *Evening Post.* 23 September 1976.

Jacobs, Nancy. "Lowcountry Intrigues Folklorist." *Post/Courier.* 23 October 1977.

"Jannie Gourdine." *Post/Courier.* 26 October 1980.

Jarrell, Frank P. "Exhibit examines sweetgrass basketry." *Post/Courier.* 7 September 1986.

"The Knack." *News and Courier.* 8 November 1977.

Koonse, Christie. "Take a Treat Home." *Post/Courier. 3*0 March 1980.

Leland, Jack. "Basket Weaving African Art Survival?" *News and Courier.* 27 March 1949.

Leland, Jack. "Two Local Basket Weavers Demonstrate Art in Canada." *News and Courier.* 21 July 1971.

Lione, Louise. "The Basket Weavers of Charleston." *Charlotte Observer.* 22 June 1986.

"Local Baskets on Exhibit at Smithsonian," *News and Courier,* 8 December 1977.

Locklair, Ernie. "Ancient Art on Display." *News and Courier.* 21 July 1974.
Locklair, Margaret. "New Program Markets State Handcrafts." *News and Courier.* 1 May 1977.

_____. "Handcraft Guild." *Evening Post.* 6 May 1977.

Lofton, Sally. "A Primitive Art Thrives." *News and Courier.* 12 August 1962.

"Lowcountry Art." *Post/Courier.* 18 November 1984.

"Lowcountry Arts Again Get National Recognition." *Evening Post.* 8 December 1977.

"Lowcountry Basket Exhibit on Display." *Post/Courier.* 27 May 1984.

"Maggie Mazyck, Flower Vendor, Dies At 83." *News and Courier.* 24 January 1961.

"Market Visitors." *Post/Courier.* 8 May 1977.

McDowell, Elsa F. "Mary Foreman Jackson Weaves Works of Art." *Post/Courier.* 9 December 1984.

Montgomery, Claude A. "Lowcountry Basket Weavers." *The State Magazine.* Columbia, S.C. 9 August 1953.

"Mt. Pleasant Woman Discusses Gullah Basket Craft at N.C. Fair." *Evening Post.* 20 September 1979.

Murphy, Edward D. "Lowcountry Artisans Chosen for National Award." *News and Courier.* 7 September 1984.

"Native Basket Weaving." *News and Courier.* 15 May 1963.

Nellis, Kathleen. "Artists Demonstrate Native Crafts." *Post/Courier.* 18 March 1979.

"New Group Will Aid Foreign Guests Here." *News and Courier.* 28 March 1962.

"Oil Painting Captures Flavor of Old Market, Charleston Square (oil painting) by Charles J. Hamilton." *News and Courier.* 11 August 1974.

"Old City Market Remains a Symbol of Traditions." *News and Courier.* 28 September 1959.

Owens, J. Walker. "Tourist Business Comprises Big Industry for Charleston." *News and Courier.* April 1948.

Pertuit, T. Edward. "Negro Weavers' Art Part of Lowcountry." *News and Courier.* 20 November 1961.

Pugh, Betty. "Ancient Art of Weaving Baskets Catches Eyes of Tourists Here." *News and Courier.* 4 April 1953.

Roberts, Nancy. "Gullah Baskets." *Americana* 7:1(March 1979): 38-41.

Rozin, Skip. "The Handmade Baskets of Charleston." *New York Times.* 13 February 1983.

Sadler, Betty. "'People Stop and Talk; Some Buy—Some Don't,'" *The State.* 11 March 1966.

Salinger, Wendy. "Lowcountry Crafts." *Gateway Magazine.* Charleston, S.C. August 1978.

Scroggins, Elizabeth McRae. "Gullah Baskets." *ETV Guide.* Columbia, S.C. 1 April 1971.

"Sea Grass Basket Weavers: Coastal Negroes Produced Artistic Effects in Useful Articles." *Coastal Topics.* Charleston, S.C. April, 1937.

"A Selective Listing of Lowcountry Trends and Events." *Post/Courier.* 5 August 1979.

"Sierra Leone has S.C. Ties," *Post/Courier.* 5 January 1986.

Small, Robert. "Basket Weavers D.C.-Bound." *News and Courier.* 16 October 1979.

_____. "Basket Weavers." *News and Courier.* 7 November 1979.

Smith, Charlotte. "The Last of the Old-Time Basket Makers." *Savannah News.* 17 July 1960.

Smith, Fran. "Daufuskie 'mayor' loves island's peacefulness." *The Island Packet.* Hilton Head, S.C. 4 February 1982.

Sneed, Judith Rhodes. "Basket Makers." [Letters to the Editor] *Evening Post.* 11 May 1977.

Sparkman, Mary A. "Charleston's Street Vendors." *News and Courier.* 3 March 1963.

Speight, Carol. "The Creative Hand." *South Carolina Wildlife.* (July-August 1977): 40-41.

Stracener, William. "Weaver Will Weave 'Until the Day I Die'." *The State.* n.d. LSC.

"Sunshine and Sweetgrass." *News and Courier.* 14 March 1984.

"Sweetgrass Baskets." *Evening Post.* 23 March 1983.

"Symmetry of Straw." *News and Courier.* 4 October 1977.

Taylor, Bill. "Baskets." *The Fairfield Independent.* 19, 26 July 1979.

"Tourist Business History Traced." *News and Courier.* 6 April 1939.

"Two Area Residents Are in Crafts Fair." *Evening Post.* 17 August 1977.

"Two Showings Set for Weavers' Special." *News and Courier.* 24 April 1971.

"A Visit to the Basketmakers." *News and Courier.* 17 November 1984.

"Vote of Approval." *News and Courier.* 9 September 1977.

Wallace, Sue. "Times Features Gullah Art." *Evening Post.* 17 April 1975.

Waring, Thomas R., Jr. "Grass Weavers in Four-Mile Area Make Unique Product." *News and Courier.* 15 November 1936.

Weber, Meryl. "Gullah Baskets." *Arts and Activities.* 84:4 (December, 1978): _____.

Weintraub, Boris. "Just An Incredible Country We Live In." *Arts Review* 2:1(Fall, 1984): 14-18.

"When Buzzards Were Scavengers in Market Street." *Evening Post.* 26 July 1939.

Williams, Barbara S. "Basketmakers Given Help in Getting Sweet Grass." *News and Courier.* 29 July 1972.

"Would You Take. . . ." *News and Courier.* 17 May 1977.

IV. Books, Dissertations, and Journal Articles

Allen, William Francis, Charles Pickard Ware and Lucy McKim Garrison. *Slave Songs of the United States.* 1867. Reprint. New York: Peter Smith, 1951.

Allston, R.F.W. *Essay of Sea Coast Crops.* Charleston: A.E. Miller, 1854. SCL.

Annual Reports of the Penn Normal, Industrial, and Agricultural School, 1910-1951. SCL.

Blassingame, John. *Slave Testimony: Two Centuries of Letters, Speeches, Interviews, and Autobiographies.* Baton Rouge: Louisiana State University Press, 1977.

Burton, Richard F. *Wit and Wisdom From West Africa: Or a Book of Proverbial Philosophy, Idioms, Enigmas, and Laconisms.* 1865. Reprint. New York: Biblio and Tanner, 1969.

Chabreck, R.H., and R.E. Condrey. *Common Vascular Plants of the Louisiana Marsh.* Baton Rouge: Louisiana State University Center for Wetland Resources, December, 1979.

Chase, Judith Wragg. *Afro-American Art and Craft.* New York: Van Nostrand Reinhold Co., 1971.

Clifton, James M. "Golden Grains of White: Rice Planting on the Lower Cape Fear." *The North Carolina Historical Review* 50:4 (October 1973): 365-393.

_____, ed. *Life and Labor on Argyle Island: Letters and Documents of a Savannah River Rice Plantation, 1833-1867.* Savannah: The Beehive Press, 1978.

Cooley, Rossa Belle. *Homes of the Freed.* 1926. Reprint. New York: Negro Universities Press, 1970.

Dabbs, Edith M. *Face of an Island: Leigh Richmond Miner's Photographs of St. Helena Island.* Columbia: The R.L. Bryan Co., 1970.

Davis, Gerald L. "Afro-American Coil Basketry in Charleston County, South Carolina," in *American Folklife,* edited by Don Yoder, pp. 151-184. Austin: University of Texas Press, 1976.

"Egg-Shaped" Basket (cat. 53)

Day, Gregory. "Afro-Carolinian Art, Towards the History of a Southern Expressive Tradition." *Contemporary Art/Southeast* 1:5 (January/February 1978): 10-21.

Day, Kay Young [Kate Porter Young]. "My Family Is Me: Women's Kin Networks and Social Power in a Black Sea Island Community." Ph.D. dissertation, Rutgers University, 1983.

Derby, Doris Adelaide. "Afro-American Baskets." *World Heritage Museum Notes* 3 (1976).

_____, "Black Women Basket Makers: "A Study of Domestic Economy in Charleston County, South Carolina." Ph.D. dissertation, University of Illinois, 1980.

Doar, David. *A Sketch of the Agricultural Society of St. James, Santee, South Carolina and an Address on the Traditions and Reminiscences of the Parish Delivered before Society on 4th of July 1907.* Charleston: Calder-Fladger Co., 1908.

_____. *Rice and Rice Planting in the South Carolina Lowcountry.* Charleston: The Charleston Museum, 1936.

Dover, Cedric. *American Negro Art.* New York: New York Graphic Society, 1960.

Duncan, Wilbur H., and L.E. Foote. *Wildflowers of the Southeastern United States.* Athens: University of Georgia Press, 1975.

Epstein, Dena J. *Sinful Tunes and Spirituals: Black Folk Music to the Civil War.* Urbana: University of Illinois Press, 1977.

Florida Folklife Program. *Florida Basketry: Continuity and Change.* Jacksonville: Florida Department of State, 1981.

_____. *Duval County Folklife.* Jacksonville: Florida Department of State, 1985.

Foote, Henry Wilder. *The Penn School on St. Helena Island.* Reprint from Southern Workman. Hampton: Hampton Institute Press, 1904.

Hambly, Wilfred. *The Ovimbundu of Angola: Frederick H. Rawson Field Museum Ethnological Expedition to West Africa.* Chicago: Field Museum of Natural History, 1934.

Herskovits, Melville J. *The Myth of the Negro Past.* 1941. Reprint. Boston: Beacon Press, 1958.

Heyward, Duncan Clinch. *Seed From Madagascar.* Chapel Hill: University of North Carolina Press, 1937.

House, Albert Virgil, ed. *Planter Management and Capitalism in Ante-Bellum Georgia, The Journal of Hugh Fraser Grant, Ricegrower.* New York: Columbia University Press, 1954.

Irving, John B. *A Day on the Cooper River.* 1932. Reprint. Ann Arbor: University Microfilms International, 1978.

Jacoway, Elizabeth. *Yankee Missionaries in the South: The Penn School Experiment.* Baton Rouge: Louisiana State University Press, 1980.

Johnson, Guy B. *Folk Culture on St. Helena Island, South Carolina.* Chapel Hill: University of North Carolina Press, 1930.

Joyner, Charles. *Down by the Riverside: A South Carolina Slave Community.* Urbana: University of Illinois Press, 1984.

Kiser, Clyde Vernon. *Sea Island to City: A Study of St. Helena Islanders in Harlem.* New York: Columbia University Press, 1969.

Lasansky, Jeannette. *Willow, Oak, and Rye: Basket Traditions in Pennsylvania.* University Park: Penn State University Press, 1979.

Lee, Lawrence. *The Lower Cape Fear in Colonial Days.* Chapel Hill: University of North Carolina Press, 1965.

Littlefield, Daniel C. *Rice and Slaves: Ethnicity and the Slave Trade in Colonial South Carolina.* Baton Rouge: Louisiana State University Press, 1981.

Merrens, Harry Roy. *Colonial North Carolina in the 18th Century: A Study in Historical Geography.* Chapel Hill: University of North Carolina Press, 1964.

Myers, Betty. "Gullah Basketry." *Craft Horizons* 36(June, 1976): 30-31.

Parrish, Lydia. *Slave Songs of the Georgia Sea Islands.* New York: Creative Age Press, Inc., 1942.

Parsons, Elsie Clews. *Folk-Lore of the Sea Islands, South Carolina. Memoirs of the American Folk-Lore Society* 10. New York: American Folklore Society, 1923.

Peek, Philip. "Afro-American Material Culture and the Afro-American Craftsman." *Southern Folklore Quarterly* 42:2-3(1978): 109-132.

Perdue, Robert E., Jr. "'African' Baskets in South Carolina." *Economic Botany* 22:3(1968): 289-292.

Phillips, Ulrich Bonnell. *American Negro Slavery.* 1918. Reprint. Baton Rouge: Louisiana State University Press, 1966.

Pinson, Joseph N., Jr. "A Floristic Analysis of Open Dunes in South Carolina." Ph.D. dissertation, University of South Carolina, 1973.

Pinson, Joseph N., Jr., and Wade T. Batson. "The Status of Muhlenbergia Filipes Curtis (Poaceae)." *The Journal of the Elisha Mitchell Scientific Society* 87:4(Winter, 1971): 188-191.

Fruit Basket (Cat. 33)

Porcher, Francis P. *Resources of the Southern Fields and Forests.* 1863. Reprint. New York: Arno Press and the New York Times, 1970.

Powell, Richard J. "African and Afro-American Art: Call and Response." Chicago: Field Museum of Natural History, 1984.

Pringle, Elizabeth W. Allston. *Chronicles of Chicora Wood.* Boston: The Christopher Publishing House, 1940.

_____ [Pennington, Patience]. *A Woman Rice Planter.* 1913. Reprint. Cambridge: Belknap Press, 1961.

Reinecke, John E. *A Bibliography of Pidgin and Creole Languages.* Honolulu: The University Press of Hawaii, 1975.

The Rice Lands of the South." *Harper's New Monthly Magazine* 19:114(November, 1859): 721-738.

Rogers, George C., Jr. *The History of Georgetown County, South Carolina.* Columbia: University of South Carolina Press, 1970.

Rose, Willie Lee. *Rehearsal for Reconstruction.* New York: Vintage Press, 1960.

Rosenberg, Neil V., and Debora G. Kodish, eds. *"Folk-Songs of America": The Robert Winslow Gordon Collection, 1922-1932.* Washington, D.C.: The Archive of Folk Song, Library of Congress, 1978.

Rosengarten, Dale. "Spirits of Our Ancestors: Basket Traditions in the Carolinas," in *Carolina Folk: The Cradle of a Southern Tradition,* edited by George D. Terry and Lynn Robertson Myers, pp. 10-21. Columbia: McKissick Museum, The University of South Carolina, 1985.

Rosengarten, Theodore. *Tombee: Portrait of a Cotton Planter, with the Journal of Thomas B. Chaplin (1822-1890).* New York: William Morrow & Co., 1986.

Rossbach, Ed. *Baskets as Textile Art.* New York: Van Nostrand Reinhold Company, 1973.

Ruffin, Edmund. *Report of the Commencement and Progress of the Agricultural Survey of South Carolina.* Columbia: A.H. Pemberton, 1843.

Salley, Alexander S., Jr., ed. *Narratives of Early Carolina,* 1650-1708. 1911. Reprint. New York: Barnes & Noble, Inc., 1967.

Sass, Herbert Ravenel. *A Carolina Rice Plantation of the Fifties.* New York: William Morrow & Co., 1936.

Saunders, Boyd and Stephanie. *The Etchings of James Fowler Cooper.* Columbia: University of South Carolina Press, 1982.

Savannah Unit, Georgia Writers' Project, Work Projects Administration, *Drums and Shadows: Survival Studies Among the Georgia Coastal Negroes.* Athens: University of Georgia Press, 1940.

Shriner, Dorothy Sellers. "Transect Studies of Salt Marsh Vegetation in Port Royal Sound and North Edisto River Estuaries." Master's Thesis, University of South Carolina, 1971.

Sieber, Roy. *African Furniture and Household Objects.* Bloomington: Indiana University Press, 1980.

Smith, D.E. Huger. *A Charlestonian's Recollections, 1843-1913.* Charleston: Carolina Art Association, 1950.

Smith, Fred T. "Guernsi Basketry and Pottery." *African Arts* 12:1(1978): 78-81.

Smith, Julia Floyd. *Slavery and Rice Culture in Low Country Georgia, 1750-1860.* Knoxville: University of Tennessee Press, 1985.

Stampp, Kenneth M. *The Peculiar Institution: Slavery in the Ante-Bellum South.* New York: Alfred A. Knopf, 1956.

Stephenson, Sue H. *Basketry of the Appalachian Mountains.* New York: Van Nostrand Reinhold Co., 1977.

Swan, Dale Evans. *The Structure and Profitability of the Antebellum Rice Industry.* New York: Arno Press, 1975.

Teleki, Gloria Roth. *Baskets of Rural America.* New York: E.P. Dutton, 1975.

_____. *Collecting Traditional American Basketry.* New York: E.P. Dutton, 1979.

Thompson, Robert Farris. "African Influence on the Art of the United States," in *Black Studies in the University: A Symposium,* edited by Armstead L. Robinson, Craig C. Foster, and Donald H. Ogilvie. New Haven: Yale University Press, 1969.

Tindall, George Brown. *South Carolina Negroes, 1877-1900.* Columbia: University of South Carolina Press, 1952.

Trowell, Margaret, and Wachsmann, K.P. *Tribal Crafts of Uganda.* London: Oxford University Press, 1953.

Twining, Mary A. "An Examination of African Retentions in the Folk Culture of the South Carolina and Georgia Sea Islands." Ph.D. dissertation, Indiana University, 1977.

_____. "Harvesting and Heritage: A Comparison of Afro-American and African Basketry." *Southern Folklore Quarterly* 42:2-3(1978): 159-174.

_____. "Sea Island Basketry: Reaffirmations of West Africa," in *The First National African-American Crafts Conference: Selected Writings,* edited by David C. Driskell, pp. 35-39. Memphis: Shelby State Community College, 1980.

Vlach, John M. *The Afro-American Tradition in Decorative Arts.* Cleveland: The Cleveland Museum of Art, 1978.

_____. "Arrival and Survival: The Maintenance of an Afro-American Tradition of Folk Art and Craft," in *Perspectives on American Folk Art,* edited by Ian M. G. Quimby and Scott T. Swank, pp. 177-217. New York: W. W. Norton & Co., 1980.

Wigginton, Eliot, ed. *The Foxfire Book.* Garden City: Doubleday & Co., 1972.

Wood, Peter H. *Black Majority: Negroes in Colonial South Carolina from 1670 through the Stono Rebellion.* New York: Alfred A. Knopf, 1974.

_____. "'It Was a Negro Taught Them:' A New Look At Labor in Early South Carolina." *Journal of Asian and African Studies* 9(1974): 159-179.

Woofter, T. J., Jr. *Black Yeomanry: Life on St. Helena Island.* New York: Henry Holt & Co., 1930.

Wright, James Leitch, Jr. *The Only Land They Knew: The Tragic Story of the American Indians in the Old South.* New York: The Free Press, 1981.

Basketmakers Interviewed
in the Lowcountry Basket Project

Mary Jane and Jessie Bennett, Mt. Pleasant, S.C.
Mae Bell Coakley, Mt. Pleasant, S.C.
Jannie Cohen, Hilton Head Island, S.C.
Annabell Ellis, Mt. Pleasant, S.C.
Evelyina and Joseph Foreman, Mt. Pleasant, S.C.
Yvonne Foreman, Mt. Pleasant, S.C.
Florence Frazier, Baltimore, Md.
Helen and James Gadsden, Awendaw, S.C.
Laverne Gadsden, Awendaw, S.C.
Sandra Gadsden, Awendaw, S.C.
Allen and Annie Mae Green, Sapelo Island, Ga.
Mary Jackson, Charleston, S.C.
Frances Jones, Hilton Head Island, S.C.
Maggie Manigault, Mt. Pleasant, S.C.

Marie Manigault, Mt. Pleasant, S.C.
Mary Jane Manigault, Mt. Pleasant, S.C.
Melony Manigault, Mt. Pleasant, S.C.
Florence Mazyck, Mt. Pleasant, S.C.
Rosemarie Mazyck, Awendaw, S.C.
Barbara McCormick, McClellanville, S.C.
Sue Middleton, Mt. Pleasant, S.C.
April Rivers, Charleston, S.C.
Sharod Carlton Rouse, Cartersville, Ga.
Latoyana Scott, Mt. Pleasant, S.C.
Mary Alice Scott, Mt. Pleasant, S.C.
Meggan Scott, Mt. Pleasant, S.C.
Michelle Scott, Sumter, S.C.
Tiffany Scott, Mt. Pleasant, S.C.
Adam and Lilly Singleton, Frogmore, S.C.
Henrietta Snype, Mt. Pleasant, S.C.
Mary Vanderhorst, Mt. Pleasant, S.C.
Blanche Watts, Mt. Pleasant, S.C.
Louise White, Awendaw, S.C.
Mary White, Awendaw, S.C.

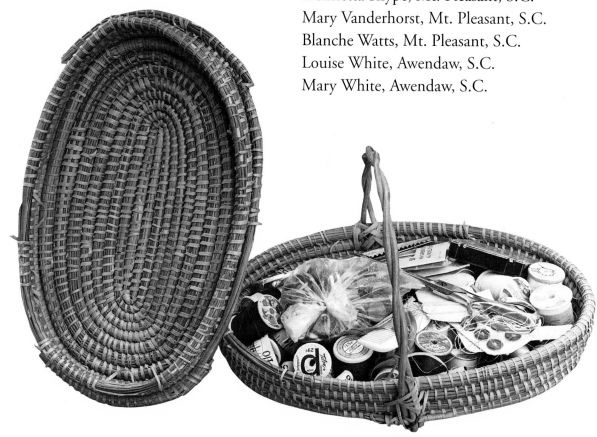

The Folk Arts Program
McKissick Museum

McKissick Museum was founded in 1976, bringing together several subject museums at the University of South Carolina into a single organization. The Museum is named for J. Rion McKissick, the President of the University of South Carolina in the late 1930s, who oversaw the construction of the building at the east end of the historic Horseshoe of the Columbia campus which the Museum now occupies. Since its founding, McKissick Museum has sought to provide exhibitions, lectures series, and conferences that put South Carolinians in touch with their own heritage. Besides serving the community with exhibitions in the arts, history, and geology of South Carolina, three award-winning exhibitions of southern folk art and many smaller exhibits were produced in the first ten years of the Museum's work.

Recognizing that these traditional arts are under-studied, yet important for our understanding of South Carolina life, the Museum began a folk arts resource center in 1985. With a grant from the National Endowment for the Arts, Folk Arts Program, a South Carolina folk arts coordinator was hired. The purpose of the resource center and the state coordinator is to identify, preserve, and promote the traditional arts of South Carolina and to serve as a source of information about southern folk arts to individuals, museums, and communities that wish to document or present their own local heritage. If you have information about the traditional arts in South Carolina—photographs, diaries, or objects of folk art, from baskets, to quilts, to stories and songs—which you wish to share with others, please contact the folk arts resource center at McKissick Museum weekdays.

McKissick Museum

Gary Stanton
South Carolina State
Folk Arts Coordinator

Sister Elizabeth Coakley's Basket Stand, Mt. Pleasant, South Carolina, 1986